WITHOUT FEAR

Dumfries Burgh Police Cap Badge

THE HISTORY
OF
THE ROYAL BURGH OF DUMFRIES POLICE
1788 - 1932

John Maxwell

A catalogue record for this book is available from the British Library and the National Library of Scotland.

ISBN 978-1-907931-48-2

Printed and bound by Solway Print, 11 Catherinefield Industrial Estate, Heathhall, Dumfries DG1 3PQ.

Dumfries Burgh Police Belt Buckle

INDEX:

Introduction:

PREFACE

I joined Dumfries and Galloway Constabulary in November 1978 and developed an interest in the history of the local force and how it grew over the years. I began the task of uncovering how it all happened. Idle curiosity to begin with followed quite quickly by dogged determination not to be beaten.

Through research I found that hundreds of people had served over the years and that rather than one force there were actually quite a number of burgh and county police forces in the region before Dumfries and Galloway Constabulary was created in 1948.

The oldest was Dumfries Burgh and even that wasn't straightforward as it developed from watchmen and burgh officers as an arm of the local council. Further to this, in my naivety, I thought it would be a good idea to chronicle as many of the officers who served with the burgh force as I could; it couldn't be that difficult, could it? Unfortunately the records are not intact and there is no list of all the officers; all the names and details have been compiled from a large number of sources from council and police records to newspaper clippings and other historical documents: and is still incomplete.

Now, to be fair, what records exist are available and the local library and archive services is staffed by a really friendly and helpful group of people, but the task I had given myself was enormous. Fifteen years later and I am still researching the history of policing Dumfries and Galloway and it's only now that I feel able to let some of my work be published and even then only as it relates to the Dumfries Burgh Police.

John Maxwell
Dumfries 2013

FOREWORD

John Maxwell had a distinguished career with Dumfries and Galloway Constabulary, which extended over a 35 year period. His final year of service, 2013, coinciding with a major change in policing when Dumfries and Galloway Constabulary was merged along with seven other police forces to form Police Scotland.

Throughout his police service John applied his natural inquisitive approach in a productive manner to the benefit of the communities he served. He also applied this approach in a different way to explore his interest in history and in particular to the history of policing in the Dumfries and Galloway area and the people who lay behind it.

His quality research identifies the embryos of 'policing' developing more than two hundred years ago and gradually forming into a range of individual forces across Dumfries and Galloway in the late 18th century. The first of these forces to form was Dumfries Burgh Police and is the focus of this book *The History of The Royal Burgh Of Dumfries Police 1788 -1932*.

History is important as it very much shapes the future and he has captured a unique insight into the social history of the area. He has focused on individual police officers, criminals, local leaders and worthies as well as key events of the time to paint a colourful and accurate picture.

As a former Chief Constable of Dumfries and Galloway Constabulary, I congratulate John Maxwell on his efforts and commend the book to others.

Patrick J Shearer, QPM

The Title, 'Without fear or favour', comes from the 'judicial oath' under the Oaths Act 1686:

"I, (name), do swear that I will well and truly serve our Sovereign Lady Queen Victoria in the office of Constable, and I will do right to all manner of people after the laws and usages of this realm, <u>without fear or favour</u>, affection or ill will. So help me God."

The phrase was also coined by Mr. R.A. Grierson, Town Clerk of Dumfries upon the sudden death of Dumfries Burgh Police Chief Constable George Stephen Lipp in 1909.

"Notwithstanding that, he was always actuated with the absolute independence and with a determination to carry out his duty, and he conceived it to be, <u>without fear or favour</u>, and moreover he did so always with a modestly and a self effacement which, he thought, was an example to them all."

Dumfries Burgh Police Tunic Button

Chapter One
PROTECTING THE BURGH and the BURGESSES

As with most royal and feudal burghs there is no specific date when the burgesses of Dumfries began policing their community.   Early policing evolved along with street cleaning, lamp lighting and watching the town gates.   Policing was a community issue; and constables were appointed and sworn into office from the freemen or burgesses of the town, and the town council appointed burgh or borough officers to act on behalf of the council, the magistrates and the justices of the peace of the burgh.

The Dumfries burgh records show that on 22nd May 1731:

> "......the said day James Clark, barber, Thomas McGowan, tailor,
> William Ewart, workman, Hugh Johnstone , lawyer, John Barbour,
> wright, Robert Gibson and David Blunt, weavers, compeared and
> appointed to office of Constable unto upon them until Whit Sunday
> next and gave their oaths defidelis and the said James Clark, Thomas
> McGowan, William Ewart, Hugh Johnstone, John Barbour, Robert
> Gibson and David Blunt...... did receive one of the town batons
> and James Dod being absent the personal summons of the Council
> recommended to the Magistrates to appoint him Constable".

The declaration of a police constable:

> The Police (Scotland) Act 1857
> "I hereby do solemnly and sincerely declare and affirm that I will
> faithfully discharge the duties of the office of constable."

The constables, once sworn in, were given a, sometimes, ornately decorated wooden baton or night stick to carry as their badge of office. Not only was this an effective and impressive method of identification, it was also a handy lump of wood to strike down any transgressors, vagabonds and rapscallions.

As with all communities in pre-Georgian times, Dumfries had no organised police force, but justice was seen to be done by the magistrates and burgh officers; and the town had its fair share of crimes, murders and public executions. The crimes varied but the outcome was invariably the same, the gibbet or the gallows.

Two remaining Dumfries Burgh Police batons with the town crest marked with 'Dumfries Burgh Police.'

Police night stick. The above stick is three feet long and has a silver cap on the end marked as Dumfries Burgh Police Fourth Ward.

A gibbet

The gallows

In 1662 at the Dumfries Court, two brothers called Irving were convicted of 'Stouthrief'. Stouthrief at that time is described as theft aggravated by the use of force and violence. The brothers were taken before the court, tried, convicted and taken to the gallows or gibbet at Marchmount which at the time was on the moor outside the town and:

"Ther to be hangit by the heid until deid."

About the same time a worthy called 'Bauld Jock' was convicted of theft of five sheep and was sentenced:

"To be drowned till he be deid in the watter of the Nith."

Death by drowning was considered to be a more humane; and a sentence of lesser severity than hanging and was regularly used for executing those accused of witchcraft. The location and manner of this execution is unknown, although execution by drowning was generally carried out by tying the accused to a post, or seat, below the high water mark and letting the natural flow of tidal water overcome them and drown them.

In 1733 a local gypsy called John Johnstone, was tried and convicted of robbery and accessory to murder. In 1860 the Rev. Dr. Alexander Carlyle (1722-1805) was a witness and reported on the event as follows:-

*"There was one Jock Johnstone who had been condemned for robbery,
and, being accessory to a murder, to be executed at Dumfries. This
fellow was but twenty years of age, but strong and bold, and a great
ringleader. It was strongly reported that the thieves were collecting in*

all quarters, in order to come to Dumfries on the day of the execution, and make a deforcement as they were conducting Jock to the gallows, which was usually erected on a muir (moor) out of town. The magistrates became anxious; and there being no military force nearer than Edinburgh, they resolved to erect the gallows before the door of the prison, with a scaffold or platform leading from the door to the fatal tree, and they armed about one hundred of their stoutest burgesses with Lochaber axes to form a guard round the scaffold. The day and hour of execution came, and I was placed in the window of the provost's house directly opposite the prison: the crowd was great, and the preparations alarming to a young imagination: at last the prison-door opened, and Jock appeared, enclosed by six town-officers. When he first issued from the door, he looked a little astonished; but looking round a while, he proceeded with a bold step. Psalms and prayers being over, the rope was fastened about his neck, and he was prompted to ascend a short ladder fastened to the gallows, to be thrown off. Here his resistance and my terror began. Jock was curly-haired and fierce-looking, and very strong of his size — about five feet eight inches. The moment they asked him to go up the ladder, he took hold of the rope round his neck, which was fastened to the gallows, and, with repeated violent pulls, attempted to pull it down; and his efforts were so strong that it was feared he would have succeeded. The crowd, in the mean time, felt much emotion, and the fear of the magistrates increased. I wished myself on the top of Criffel, or anywhere but there. But the attempt to go through the crowd appeared more dangerous than to stay where I was, out of sight of the gallows. I returned to my station again, resolving manfully to abide the worst extremity.

Jock struggled and roared, for he became like a furious wild beast, and all that six men could do, they could not bind him; and having with wrestling hard forced up the pinions on his arms, they were afraid, and he became more formidable; when one of the magistrates, recollecting that there was a master mason or carpenter, of the name of Baxter, who was by far the strongest man in Dumfries, they with difficulty prevailed with him, for the honour of the town, to come on the scaffold. He came, and, putting aside the six men who were keeping him down, he seized him, and made no more difficulty than a nurse does in handling her child: he bound him hand and foot in a few minutes, and laid him quietly down on his face near the edge of the scaffold, and retired. Jock, the moment he felt his grasp, found himself subdued, and became calm, and resigned himself to his fate. This dreadful scene cost me many nights' sleep."

In 1753 Robert McIlymont was hanged for horse theft. The exact location of the hanging is not recorded, but, like in 1662 it is believed to have been on the moor at Marchmount.

In 1763 Thomas Price a soldier broke into Wilson's Shop in Dumfries and stole a number of pocket watches. He was tried, convicted and hanged for theft by housebreaking.

While in 1780 William Johnston an innkeeper and postmaster at Moffat was tried and hanged at Dumfries for intercepting the post and then stealing bank notes from the mail.

1787 saw the execution of William Richardson for the gruesome murder of his partner. Richardson murdered Elizabeth Hughan his 19 year old girlfriend whilst she was seven months pregnant with his child.

In April, 1789 a letter was received by the Sheriff at Dumfries:

".....The Sheriff of the County of Dumfries has received a letter from Lord Sydney, containing orders to send the convicts under sentence of transportation from the prison of Dumfries to Plymouth.

And yesterday another letter arrived, containing pardons for Winlock and Afflect under sentence of death. These unhappy men are banished during life, and their service adjudged for seven years."

John Carmichael a 22 year old Soutar or shoemaker was hanged in 1789 for theft by housebreaking. His co-accused Robert Leggat had also been convicted and sentenced to death but was later reprieved and Carmichael went to the gallows alone.

At the time, the Dumfries Weekly Journal followed the case with great interest:

"DUMFRIES 6th January 1789

Some days ago two men of the name Ligget and Carmichael, were apprehended for breaking into the warehouse of John Lauder, shopkeeper, and stealing out of it a cask, containing twenty gallons, or thereby, of British spirits. They were carried before the justices of this county; and after a long examination of themselves, and witnesses to prove their guilt, were committed to prison to stand trial for the offence before the High Court of Justiciary."

"DUMFRIES 14th April 1789

Yesterday (13th April, 1798) the Circuit Court of Justiciary was opened here by the Right Hon. Lord Justice Clerk and Lord Hailes. Same day came the trial of John Carmichael and Robert Leggat, journeymen shoemakers in Dumfries, for housebreaking and theft; and after a proof being taken the jury inclosed in the evening, and this day at ten o'clock, returned a unanimous verdict, finding both prisoners guilty.

The jury at the same time gave in a recommendation, in favour of both the prisoners, separate from their verdict, together with the reasons which induced them to recommend the prisoners to mercy. The court pronounced sentence of death against them and appointed them to be executed upon Wednesday the 27th May, next. The Lord Justice Clerk then addressed the prisoners in a very feeling manner, informing them at the same time, of the recommendation of the jury in their favour."

"DUMFRIES 2nd June.1789

On Wednesday last, John Carmichael, aged twenty two, was executed here pursuant to the sentence, for the crimes of theft and warehouse breaking. Ever since his sentence he appeared to be very serious and penitent. His behavior at the last was particularly affecting and devout. His dying declaration had been dictated every word by himself, a few days before his death. He desired to have it immediately printed; and he sent for a copy of it on the evening preceding his execution. It was his wish, by looking over it in private, to be better enabled to read the whole of it himself from the scaffold: that in opposition to all safe reports and fabricated confessions, it might appear to be his entire and genuine confession; and that coming from his own mouth at the last, it might be the more deeply affect all by whom it was heard.

He came upon the scaffold about twenty minutes past two, dressed in white: and after the clergyman by whom he was attended had prayed, he called upon all young people in particular to attend, and he read the whole of his declaration (which required a full quarter of an hour) in a manner wonderfully distinct and composed. He afterwards kneeled on the scaffold, and prayed aloud with some great fervor: and after praying some time on the ladder, was turned off about a quarter past three.

It is much to be wished, that the fate of this young man may serve as a warning to others. Both from his public declaration at the last, and from the private conversations he had with the ministers by whom he was visited, he appears to have been much misled by bad companions. With persons of this description, it is much to be regretted, that this place hath of late been much infested. But from the discoveries made by the unhappy man, it is to be hoped, that measures may hereafter be taken to detect, and to check their progress.

In the conclusion of his speech, he did in a solemn manner justify his friends, and particularly his wife, from any participation of his crimes. And it may be pleasing to the public to learn, that for this poor woman, now left destitute with three infant children, a collection was immediately begun under the direction of the Rev. Mr. Burnside, in which, by the liberal affluence of Baillie Jackson, three pounds sterling were soon obtained. This sum, which hath already been delivered to the unhappy widow, and which, it is hoped, she will manage frugally, is considerably greater, it is probable, than all the dishonest gains ever made by her husband. These indeed appear to have been so inconsiderable, that they might have easily exceeded by the honest industry of any ordinary tradesman. A striking lesson to all young persons in the same station of life, to whom industry and sobriety point out a much surer road, not only to happiness in the next world, but even to comfort in this one, than all the allurements of idleness and dishonesty."

Patrick Fitzpatrick and James Muldroch were charged, convicted and sentenced to be hanged in 1790 for theft by housebreaking. Muldroch was later reprieved and Fitzpatrick faced the gallows alone.

In 1802 a new prison was built in Buccleuch Street, Dumfries, between the present Sheriff Court and the junction with Irish Street. From 1807 all executions were carried out in public in a corner of the prison. Prior to this the town had a prison which was situated between High Street and Queensberry Square approximately where the present Santander Bank is situated.

A version of events taken from the time is related in the 'Dumfries' Story', by David Lockwood; and describes the destruction of the original Dumfries prison:

"On the 16th September 1742, Rood Fair Saturday, Provost Bell was walking down the High Street when he saw a gypsy woman steal a pair of stockings from one of the piles of goods for sale outside the shop of William Dodd, a merchant. To put your goods on the pavement was standard practice for shopkeepers, particularly on market days, as shops had small windows and were dimly lit inside. This only died out at the turn of the century. Dodd chased her and the stockings were found under her plaid. William Stewart, one of the burgh officers, took her to prison and she told John Donaldson the jailor that she was called Mary McDonald and that she came from Glasgow. As she was being locked up she begged for a piece of candle to light her to bed. There were three other prisoners on the premises at this time, one for theft and two for debt who seem to have had the run of the place. The jailor checked that everything was in order, locked up the prison and went home to bed. During the night the two debtors smelt burning and traced it to the door of the gypsy's cell.

There was no reply when they shouted and they could see through a chink in the door that the bed was on fire. They tried to raise the alarm but it was almost 11 o'clock before the jailer was roused and by this time the fire was out of control. The whole of the upper storey was ablaze and the roof timbers fell onto the streets below. The fire was so fierce that it threatened the adjacent building and there were fears for the safety of the Tolbooth which was separated from the prison only by a narrow street. The Provost ordered the charter chest to be removed to

*Baillie Dickson's shop for safe keeping, and the next day when the fire
was out he ordered a full inquiry. Only a small part of the woman's
body had not been consumed by the flames. The fire does not seem to
have spread. When the repairs were carried out, the roof was arched
with brick under the slates to make it more secure."*

On 5th November 1793 the Dumfries Weekly Journal reported:

"DUMFRIES, November...

*On Wednesday last, Michael and James Macanallie were whipt through
the streets of this town, pursuant to the sentence of the last Circuit
Court held here. – After the executioner had performed the sentence of
the law on these men, he was attacked by one of the Fencibles, (2nd.
Battalion of Breadalbane Fencibles) an Irishman, and severely beat.
The Magistrates, upon being informed of this circumstance, immediately
offered a reward for the discovery of the offender: in consequence of
which he was that evening apprehended. Next day he was delivered up
to the military, when he was tried by a court-martial, and sentenced to
receive 100 lashes, which punishment was inflicted yesterday."*

'Whipped through the streets' is a term used to denote that the convicted
person was either led tethered through the streets by a court officer or tied to
the back of a cart and then led walking through the streets. The 'executioner'
would then walk behind them whipping them as they were led through the
streets of the burgh.

On 24th November, 1795 the Dumfries Weekly Journal reported:

*"Yesterday morning, John O'Neil, late of Stoup, and Arthur O'Neil, his
son, accused of murder, were taken from the prison here to be conveyed
to Edinburgh, there to take their trial. The diet against these persons, at
the last Circuit here, was deserted 'pro loco et tempore."*

The Dumfries Sheriff Court House was constructed in 1863 on its present site
in Buccleuch Street. Designed by the architect, David Rhind, its distinctive
silhouette dominates the town's skyline even to this day. Prior to this the
court house was situated on the opposite side of the road, where the current
Municipal Chambers are sited.

The early Dumfries Town Council Chambers were on the east side of High
Street approximately where the present day Burton's and Dorothy Perkins
shop is situated in a building called the 'Tollbooth'. These new council
chambers were opened on 6th July 1727 and entrance was gained by the
'Rainbow Stairs' approximately where Old Union Street now stands. Although
the original building was built c.1473-81 on the same site and was (according
to Mr. Truckell (McDowall's Hist., 4th edition, DUM17) strengthened and

Dumfries Prison and Sheriff Courthouse, Buccleuch Street

The Tollbooth with 'Rainbow' stairs

The Coffee House Hotel

altered in 1718). There was also a 'coffee house' which was used for perusing the broadsheet newspaper of the times, 'the Caledonian Mercury', which was started in around 1660.

Dumfries has been a Royal Burgh since the twelfth century and as with all developing communities the councillors were voted for by the freeholders of each of the Wards (political divisions) of the town. It was not until 1869 that females were given the right to vote in local or municipal elections. From that date females could vote in local elections, but only if they were tax payers. The full enfranchisement of women to vote in parliamentary elections didn't occur until 1918.

From these elected councillors and the elected deans of each of the seven 'incorporated trades' of the town the council selected a provost, a number of baillies and a treasurer. The provost and the baillies also became the burgh magistrates. The magistrates ran the 'poor house', the hospital, the town jail, sat on the bench of the burgh court and generally governed or 'policed' the burgh. A new provost was elected annually as they could only serve for one year and then he had to stand down or face a fine.

Dumfries court records begin in 1506 and mostly refer to debts and assaults. It is also recorded that the faces of peat stealers were branded at the Tollbooth steps using the town key which had been heated until red hot.

In 1668 a woman was charged with 'gossiping' and was put on the 'tron' or trone. This tron was a municipal weighing machine (or post at which goods were weighed) which was situated on the Plainstanes, with the letters **"SCANDALL"'** placed on her head.

The town council appointed commissioners of police (a sub-committee of the full council) from their number and these commissioners in turn employed officers to act on behalf of the burgh. These 'burgh' or 'borough' officers carried out the day to day functions of a council collecting taxes from the residents on behalf of the 'Collector' (a council official), collecting tolls from the tonnage arriving at Dumfries harbour (the Dock Park and Kingholm Quay), drovers and travellers who passed through the town, serving warrants from the courts, arresting wrongdoers on behalf of the magistrates and justices, arresting vagrants who entered the town for appearance before the magistrates and generally ensuring that the town was a safe place to inhabit.

As regards policing the burgh, the burgh officers were eventually joined by six burgh watchmen; one for each political ward of the burgh who were sworn in as constables and were effectively the forefathers of the modern police service, although the burgh officers still had an important role to play within the community. The position of burgh officer was also recognised as a better job that a watchman and the records show that the constables applied for and often succeeded in becoming burgh officers.

The burgh officer's position was one of trust as they collected taxes and tolls on behalf of the council. They were also required to be able to read and write and act on behalf of the council serving writs and warrants. They served the justices of the peace of the burgh court and when called upon served the sheriff court as well.

Burgh officers were the general arm of the council and not only carried out all the tasks allotted to them by the council, but also by the magistrates and the Sheriff. It should be borne in mind that there was no distinction between civil and criminal court procedures at this time and magistrates, justices of the peace and sheriffs heard both civil and criminal matters at the same hearing. The vast majority of cases before the courts were for debt or petty crime.

The Dumfries Burgh justices of the peace appointed a procurator fiscal to prosecute petty crimes in the burgh court while the Dumfries county justices of the peace appointed a procurator fiscal to report on matters outwith the royal burghs. The sheriff appointed another procurator fiscal to prosecute more serious or solemn matters in the sheriff court.

Later on, during the nineteenth century, the Dumfries burgh superintendent of police was to be appointed as burgh procurator fiscal by the burgh justices to save money. He would invariably also be the inspector of weights and measures, inspector of liquor licences and inspector of ale house certificates.

Lack of sanitation, disposal of human and other waste, packs of dogs, travelling criminals, vagrants and beggars were the bane of the lives of the local people, particularly within the built up areas and burgh officers, constables and watchmen developed through time to deal with these common issues under direction from the police commissioners of the town council.

Until the 'General and Police Improvement (Scotland) Act, 1862 (25 & 26 Victoria. c.101)', there was no drainage or sewers, other than the 'gutters', burns, streams and the river that ran though the town. Bank Street (then known as Cavarts Vennel) is reputed to have been called 'that stinking vennel' by Robert Burns as disposed waste, both human and animal, flowed along the street on its way downhill onto the Lower Sandbeds (the Whitesands) and then into the River Nith. Not an edifying thought as the river was also the main supply of drinking water for the townsfolk.

'Burn Drawers' drew water from the Nith into barrels and then pushed the barrels round the streets on a cart selling the water to the residents. If you were lucky they drew the water from the north side of the town before it was contaminated by all the human and animal waste flowing down into the river. It's no surprise that the burgesses and their constables preferred to drink ale and beer rather than the water.

Robert Burns, as an officer of the excise and having moved into Ellisland Farm in 1788, would likely have known most of the Dumfries councilors when the first steps towards creating a police service was introduced. Burns's interest in politics and his intellectual curiosity would have drawn him towards the educated and ruling classes of Dumfries and there is little doubt that the local businessmen and deacons of trade that made up the town council would have fallen into that category. Burns' fame had already spread to the burgh and at the invitation of the council under the provost-ship of William Clark he had been made an honorary burgess of Dumfries in June 1787.

Notable among these early councilmen was David Staig. He was an officer of the Bank of Scotland and stood for election to the Dumfries Burgh Council successfully becoming a councillor and eventually the Provost of Dumfries. Staig was to become one of the driving forces behind the development of Dumfries from a small and unpleasant smelling market town into a respectable border capital. He and his council drove forward legislation that provided sewerage, paving, lighting and eventually policing of Dumfries.

William McDowall, (1867) tells us that in 1787 Provost David Staig and the Dumfries Burgh Council applied to Parliament for:

".....a measure to provide for the paving, cleansing, lighting and watching of the burgh, for which there had long been felt a necessity."

Parliament agreed and the Police Act was introduced:

".....the police portions of it taking effect from 1788'."

The term 'watching' is effectively the start of any organised policing in the whole of Dumfries and Galloway. What this Act meant was that Parliament agreed that the town council could levy charges against the freeholders of the burgh for providing paving, cleaning and lighting of the streets, with an extra charge being levied from 1788 when the council could start charging for 'watching' the burgh.

In an attempt to put matters into an understandable timeframe, the year that the Dumfries burgh councillors were attempting to establish a police force, Bonnie Prince Charlie was still alive.

"Prince Charles Edward Louis John Casimir Sylvester Severino Maria Stuart, born 31.12.1720 in Rome, died 31st January 1788 in Rome, was the last Stuart to claim accession to the throne of Scotland. He led the unsuccessful Jacobite Rebellion in 1745 which led to the Heritable Jurisdictions (Scotland) Act 1746 (20 Geo. II c. 43) that ended feudal and baronial law in Scotland. Nicknamed Bonnie Prince Charlie, he fled to Italy in 1776 and ended his days a broken figure abandoned by his friends and followers."

On 6th April 1787 at a meeting of the Dumfries Burgh Council, David Staig (late provost) and Mr. Aitkin the Burgh Clerk were chosen to represent the burgh at the London Parliament and argue for the passing of an Act for the collecting of taxes to procure paving, cleaning, lighting and watching over the burgh. The MP for the area was Sir James Johnstone of Westerhall and he was to notify the council when the time came for them to travel to London.

In late April, 1787, Councillor Staig travelled to London with Mr. Aitken, the Dumfries Town Clerk, where they successfully persuaded the Parliament of King George iii, to agree to an Act for the Burgh of Dumfries **(The Beer Act, 27.G.3.C.57).** This Act was costly, plus the late provost and the town clerk were away from Dumfries for several weeks. There were no overnight 'sleeper' trains or 'shuttle' flights to London in those days, travel was by foot, horse or carriage over a rutted and sometimes perilous network of tracks and roads. The whole matter cost the burgesses of Dumfries £550, a not inconsiderable sum in the 1780s considering that the annual wage for a watchman was to be about £5 per year.

The Act authorised the council to assess and collect taxes against ales and beers, together with taxing cargoes arriving at Dumfries harbour against the tonnage delivered to pay for street improvements, drainage and watchmen to guard over the burgh.

Another source of the origin of the police in Dumfries is the 3rd Statistical Account of Scotland, (George Houston, Collins, Glasgow, 1962) which reported that:

"An original Police Force was established in the Burgh of Dumfries in 1788."

From this and other evidence there can be little doubt that some form of policing was introduced in 1788, although it was carried out by 'night watchmen' and burgh officers and burgesses appointed to act as constables under the control of the superintendents of police rather than an especially designated police service. This is unfortunate, as had a police force been created then it would have been the earliest police force in the United Kingdom. The earliest UK police force is now recognised as the Glasgow City Police, having been formed in 1800.

More importantly, from the council's perspective, they had parliamentary approval to collect taxes to improve the paving, cleansing, lighting and watching of the burgh and it is likely that street improvements were as high on their agenda as that of watchmen.

This type of legislation was being introduced across the whole nation with roads, drainage, lighting and bridges being constructed from London to Aberdeen. Every one of these roads and bridges required an act of parliament to empower the local authority to assess and collect a tax to pay for the construction.

Dumfries at this time centred on the Market Place or Plainstanes, the area immediately to the south of the Midsteeple. The town effectively took in what is now Buccleuch Street to St Michael's Church and from the Whitesands to what is now Loreburn Street and Queens Street. The west side of the river consisted of Brigend, (later to become Maxwelltown) which was in the Stewartry of Kirkcudbright and not part of Dumfries, or for that matter, Dumfriesshire.

The extreme south side of the town was at Kirkgate (St Michael Street). There was no St Michael's Bridge and no Brooms Road. Access to Cresswell Hill was via Barnslaps. There was a moorland fed from the Mill Burn which ran into the River Nith at the area where suspension Bridge now stands. The Lore Burn ran southwards from Catherine Street where the Ewart Library now sits into the Mill Burn.

Mill Gate (Burns Street) led from the Kirkgate to Shakespeare Street. Irish Street, led north and Soutargate (Soutar is old Scots for a cobbler) (the south part of High Street) led up the hill to the Market Place. Shakespeare Street led up to the Lochmabengate (English Street). The Lower Sandbeds (Whitesands) was a sandy bay running alongside the River Nith with no discernible roadway. There was a ford just north of where the suspension bridge is now situated as to cross Devorgilla Bridge you had to pay a toll.

Friars Vennel led from the Devorgilla Bridge up to the what was colloquially known as Townhead (Burn's Statue). Cavart's Vennel (Bank Street) led from the Whitesands onto the High Road (High Street) and the Fleshmarket or Back Raw (Queensberry Street) led from the Market Place to the Townhead (Burns Statue).

The Market Place was on the Plainstanes at the Midsteeple. The Yairdheids (Loreburn Street) led from Lochmabengate (English Street) to Townhead Port (Academy Street). Queen Street was a recent development as was Great King Street.

There were none of the wide and airy pedestrian passageways that we see now, but narrow alleyways called vennels or closes. Lots of people crammed into small unhygienic living spaces, throwing their waste out onto the street below.

On 9th October 1787 the commissioners of police of Dumfries were elected from the town council. These 'Commissioners for the Common Council' consisted of David Staig, Francis Maxwell, John Lawson, John Hutton, William Boyd, William Nelson, Robert Jackson (Publisher of the newspaper of the time, The Dumfries Weekly News) and James Primrose and they were appointed for one year.

The council met in the Council Chambers at the Tollbooth, which was situated on the first floor of the Rainbow Stairs in High Street Dumfries. Access to the council chambers was via a lane (Old Union Street) which is situated approximately between what is now High Street and Queensberry Street to the north side of the present Burton the Tailor Shop.

From this transitional point in time they were to appoint a superintendent of police. The superintendent of police would be a councillor or council official and not a police officer as we understand it today. Policing the burgh was a generic term for local government and looking after the town and the townsfolk. The superintendent of police also presided over street cleaning , which was carried out by 'scavengers', lamp lighting, bell ringing, paving, sanitation and sundry other matters that came under the heading 'police'.

When the time came to introduce burgh constables the council met and selected their commissioners of police. In addition to these commissioners were a group of independent individuals who represented the local community.

On Tuesday 14th October 1788 the following attended at a meeting of the Dumfries Town Council:

David Staig, Provost, William Boyd, Baillie, John Lawson, Baillie Robert Jackson, Baillie Francis Maxwell, Town Treasure, James Primrose, Convener of the Trades, William Clark, late Provost, William Hutton, late Baillie John Hutton, Merchant.

Appointed from the community were:

Robert Maxwell, late Provost, Robert Ramsey, writer, William Hyslop of Lochend, John Key, merchant, Thomas Crosbie, merchant, William Wilson of Pannerhill and William McGhie, late Convener of the Trades.

From this meeting William Boyd, John Lawson and Robert Ramsey were appointed as superintendents of police.

Law enforcement at this time was not an easy task, there were no communications systems and little or no back up should things go wrong. A disastrous example of this was on 28th March 1788 when eight officers of the customs and excise asked for, but were refused assistance by the dragoons quartered at Dumfries and set out from the town for Crawfordjohn unaided. About 1am on the Monday morning they arrived at Crawfordjohn and found and seized six contraband boxes of tea and ten bales of tobacco.

No sooner had they seized the contraband than they were set upon by a large group of smugglers assisted by a mob from the local neighbourhood, all armed with pistols, sticks, stones and other offensive weapons. The excise men were forced to withdraw with their wounded as they were heavily outnumbered and the contraband was reclaimed by the smugglers.

The problems with waste, both human and animal, didn't go away with the advent of street improvements and watchmen. While council employees called 'scavengers' cleaned up most of the rubbish and other waste from the town, the disposal of animal and human dung was still a serious problem.

As a result on 20th October 1789 the Dumfries Weekly Journal published the following advertisement for a contractor to bid for clearing the streets of the manure:

"DUNG

The set of the cleaning the Street of this Borough for the ensuing year, from the 22nd of November 1789, is to be made by public roup, (auction) by the commissioners of Police, upon Thursday the 5th November 1789, at mid-day, in the Council Chambers.

The streets are to be divided into two lots, viz. the one from Bank Street and Lochmabengate (English Street), up to the Town-head (Burns Statute); and the other from these Streets down to the Catstrand (Catstrand means small stream).

The commissioners have reason to believe, that if the Dung was neatly collected, it would amount to at least one thousand cart loads. And in a wet season to not under twelve hundred cart loads: of course it becomes a great object for the neighbouring farmers.

The articles of roup to be seen in the hands of Hugh McCornock, jun. Clerk to the Commissioners."

The Royal Burgh of Dumfries was in a period of transition and financial growth. This is exemplified by the opening of the six hundred seated, Theatre Royal in 1790. The building was planned and constructed by Boyd and Phipps. The theatre still stands as a working theatre today and, at the time of writing, is to undergo a major reconstruction and modernisation programme.

In 1791 a new stone bridge was built between Dumfries and Brigend (Maxwelltown). Thomas Boyd designed and built a five arch bridge spanning the River Nith between Buccleuch Street and Galloway Street. Brigend (later to become Maxwelltown) is described as a lawless, notorious and barbarous place with no justice, law, police or courts.

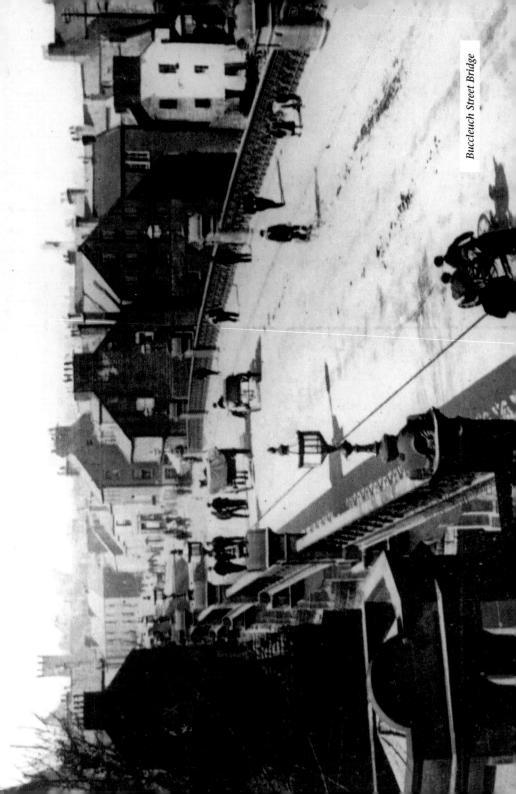

Buccleuch Street Bridge

The Dumfries horse races were also a popular feature at this time. Run over a race course at Tinwald Downs. The racing was all part of the social scene of the time and it's reported on 30th October 1792 that the noblemen and gentlemen in attendance subscribed towards the building of a new prison for Dumfries, raising £510, an astonishing sum for the times.

On 18th September 1792 the Dumfries Weekly Journal showed the following:

"PRISON BROKE

Whereas upon Wednesday night or Thursday morning last, THOMAS WILSON, who was sentenced to be transported beyond seas for fourteen years, made his escape from the Tollbooth of Dumfries. He is about 40 years of age, five feet six inches high, thick made, dark coloured hair, white faced, and his left eye remarkably small. He had on a blue coat (Scots cloth) with white metal buttons, a green shag or plush waistcoat, brownish coloured corduroy breeches, and white yarn stockings.

Whoever will apprehend the said Thomas Wilson, and secure him in any of His Majesty's jails in Great Britain, shall receive a reward of Ten Guineas from the Magistrates of Dumfries

Dumfries, Sept. 18th, 1792."

On 30th October 1792 the following advertisement appeared in the Dumfries Weekly Journal:

"WANTED:
Two stout and sober men of good character for borough officers and one for council officer. The persons inclining to accept these offices may apply to the Magistrates."

In April 1793 the magistrates and council of Dumfries came to a resolution to augment the salaries of the 'borough officers', to eight pounds per annum and they were inclined to accept applications to the magistrates for three additional officers from those who could be recommended for 'sobriety, honesty and steadiness'.

At the same time the following was reported in the Dumfries Weekly Journal:

"Whereas on Wednesday night the 3rd of April current, a woman, called Sarah Weems, laid down an infant child of hers at the house of Samuel Walker, labourer here, and has since absconded. She is above 30 years of age, about five feet high, with pale hair, and a ruddy complexion. The Magistrates hereby offer a Reward of ONE GUINEA to any person that will apprehend and secure her, so that she may be dealt with as the law directs."

While we may complain about taxation, in 1797, Alex Menzies, Head Distributor and Collector, North Britain, placed the following in the local Dumfries Weekly Journal:

"HAIR POWDER TAX

Stamp Office, Edinburgh, 25th May, 1797

Notice is Hereby Given, THAT the HAIR POWDER CERTIFICATES, will now be given out at this office, and the respective offices in North Britain, formerly advertised, to all persons who may begin to wear Hair Powder during the year, on Wednesday only, from ten o'clock forenoon till three afternoon.

Every person wearing hair Powder since 5th April last, and neglecting to take out a certificate, forfeits TWENTY POUNDS.

Several householders having neglected to return lists of persons resident in their houses, liable to the duty for the year from April 1796 to April last, in terms of the requisitions made to them by the Surveyors of Taxes, whereby they have forfeited TWENTY POUNDS: Prosecutions will be commenced for recovery of these forfeitures, against every Householder liable therein, who shall not have returned Lists to the Surveyors of taxes, in terms of the requisitions made to them, on or before the 18th June next."

On 29th February 1798 a local merchant and councilor, John Hutton, was appointed superintendent of police. His responsibilities ranged from supervising the burgh officers, ensuring that the scavenging (collection of rubbish and manure) was undertaken and that the street lighting, bell ringing and toll collecting were taking place.

Such was the range and extent of the duties of the burgh officers; it is reported that in 1798 two burgh officers were dismissed for refusing to cut down the bodies of two men hanged on the burgh gibbet. The only local execution during that year was reported in the Dumfries Weekly Journal:

"13th November 1798

On Wednesday last, David and Joseph McRobert, brothers, were executed here pursuant to their sentence, for the crime of housebreaking and theft - since their condemnation, they have professed great contrition and penitence; and, at the place of execution, behaved in a manner becoming men in their awful situation."

Dismissal was to become a common occurrence for the early policemen as any infraction of the strict disciplinary codes was met with extreme disapproval from their council masters. However they were usually re-employed again as there was a limited number of men available who could read and write and were prepared to carry out the tasks.

During February 1803 the English press reported the following:

"The following Story Shews the Danger of trusting to Circumstantial Evidence:

About forty years ago, at one of the provincial assizes, a Gentleman was tried and convicted, upon circumstantial evidence, of the murder of his niece. The circumstances sworn to were as follows: that the uncle and niece were seen walking in the fields; that a person at a small distance definitely heard the niece exclaim, "Don't kill me, uncle! Don't kill me!" and that instantly a pistol or fowling piece was fired off. Upon these circumstances the Gentleman was convicted and executed. Near twelve months after, the niece, who had eloped, arrived in England, and hearing of the affair, elucidated the whole transaction. It appeared that she had formed an attachment for a person whom her uncle disapproved; when walking in the fields, he was earnestly dissuading her from the connection, when she replied that she was resolved to have him, or it would be her death, and therefore said, "Don't kill me uncle! Don't kill me!" At the moment of uttering these words, a fowling piece was discharged by a sportsman in a neighbouring field. The same night she eloped from her uncle's house and the combination of those suspicious circumstances occasioned his ignominious death."

The following extract is taken from a council meeting on 24th May 1803 when Superintendent John Hutton's position was extended to include the superintendence of public works;

"The said day the magistrates and councillors having taken into consideration that many of the public works belonging to and carried on by them, have of late been very much neglected to the great risk and prejudice of the town and that the commissioners of Police have appointed John Hutton, merchant in Dumfries, to Superintend the Police of the town in so far as they are concerned the magistrates and Council therefore approving of what the commissioners of Police have done, they in like manner appoint the said, John Hutton, to Superintend the Public Works of and belonging to the town, conform to particular instruction given to him by the commissioners of Police, with a salary of ten pounds sterling annually."

In September 1803, the Town Council placed the following advertisement in the 'Journal':

"WANTED

Four stout men as WATCHMEN for the Town Guard of Dumfries. They will receive good encouragement, by applying to Provost Richardson."

Those standing for public office used the 'Journal' to intimate their interest in vacant positions:

"Custom House, Dumfries, 5th February 1805.

To the commissioners of Supply for the County of Dumfries and Stewartry of Kirkcudbright.

Gentlemen
Being encouraged by several respectable friends, to offer myself as a Candidate to succeed the late Mr. Hugh McCornock, as COLLECTOR of the ROAD MONEY for the District of the County of Dumfries, comprehending the parishes of Dumfries, Caerlaverock, Kirkmahoe, Kirkmichael, and Tinwald; and the District of Kirkbean, Newabbey, Troqueer, Lochmaben, Irongray, and Terregles, in the Stewartry - May I beg leave to solicit the favour of your vote and friendship, on the day of Election, which I understand to be on the 30th April next.   And I venture to assure you, that every attention on my part shall be exerted to obtain your approbation.
I am respectfully,
GENTLEMEN
Your most humble Servant
Jas. Locke."

On the 11th of September 1807 Maitland Smith a stocking maker was tried at Dumfries for the murder of Alex Williamson.

"Smith a native of Penpont and successful businessman had fallen on hard times after an initially prosperous period. He embezzled £25 from the Mutual Aid Society, of which he was treasurer, and in an act of madness shot and killed Alexander Williamson during a bungled robbery near Kirkgunzeon. He was later convicted at Dumfries Court and publicly hanged at Dumfries Prison."

Henry Duncan's 'The Young South Country Weaver.' Includes the story of Maitland Smith.

On 27th October 1807 the 'Journal' report of his execution was as follows:

"On Wednesday last, MAITLAND SMITH, who had at our last circuit court, been found guilty of the complicated crimes of murder and robbery, was executed here in the presence of a great concourse of people.

On the scaffold he displayed degree of composure and fortitude which astonished every spectator. With a firm and audible voice, he read a printed speech which he had composed for the occasion, in which he explained in the strongest terms, the sense he entertained of the enormity of his guilt, and earnestly recommended his wife and infant children to the protection of the public. He then addressed himself to the crowd in an animated and affecting manner, and continued his exhortations even after the fatal noose was round his neck. To the last he was firm and collected, and seemed to be supported in this trying scene by the hope of a pardon through a crucified redeemer: - We understand that an account of his life is in a few days to be published, for the benefit of his widow and children, which will contain some very curious and interesting particulars; and even independently of the charitable motive for which it is undertaken, will probably be found worthy the attention of the public."

In 1810 Brigend became Maxwelltown, when Marmaduke Constable Maxwell of Terregles obtained a 'Charter' from the Crown making the village a Burgh of Barony; allowing the small town to have its own provost, council, court and police. Maxwell also took the opportunity to name the new burgh after himself. Maxwelltown never had a large police force and usually consisted of a superintendent of police and one or two constables. The surrounding rural area was to be policed by the Stewartry police force.

On 18th September 1810 the Dumfries and Galloway Courier reported on the election results:

"MAXWELLTOWNE ELECTION

The village of Bridgend of Dumfries was lately erected into a free and independent Burgh of Barony, by a Charter of Maxwelltowne, and to be governed by a provost, two baillies, and four councillors, chosen annually on the eleventh day of September, by the Burgesses; and on Tuesday last the first election took place, when the following Gentlemen were elected into office:

PHILIP FORSYTH, Esq.	*Provost.*
Messrs. Robert Crawford:	*Baillie*
William Hyslop:	*Baiilie*
William Philips:	*Baillie*
James Locke:	*Councillor*
James Anderson:	*Councillor*
James Smith:	*Councillor.*

After the election, the Magistrates, Councillors, a number of the Burgesses, and several Gentlemen from the neighbourhood, who

honoured them with their presence, dined together, and the greatest
harmony and good order prevailed.

The inhabitants, in order to shew their joy upon the occasion, kindled
bonfires, and paraded the streets in the evening, with colours, drums
and fifes; and, in fact, we have not witnessed a more regular and joyful
assembly of the populace."

In 1811 the original Act that created the Dumfries police was re-enforced by
another Act for Paving, Cleaning, Lighting and Watching the Streets and
otherwise regulating the police of the town of Dumfries, passed in the 27th
year of the reign of his Majesty, King George 111'.

At a meeting of the Police commissioners on 17th June 1811, the town was
sub divided into six political wards under terms of the new Act:

"Ward 1:
The head of the town and include both sides of Townhead Street
(Burns Statue), both sides of Fleshmarket Street to Queensberry Square,
terminating at the north corner of the square with the old 'Beehive'
Close on the one side and the corner shop, nearly opposite the said
Beehive Close, possessed by John Mclellan, on the other. And including
both side of High Street, from the Townhead, and including the north
side of Rotten Row, both sides of Castle Street, both sides of Buccleuch
Street to the bridge, Charlotte Street and the new projected streets
through Clerk Maxwell's and the late Riddel's property with all the
intermediate lanes and buildings.

Ward 2
The second ward shall comprehend the whole of Friars Vennel and Saint
David's Street on both sides, with Bell's Wynde the whole of old Brewery
Street and new Bridge Street, including the several lanes or passages
connecting those streets, and terminating at the White sands and
including the east side of the said Sands to Hodgson's House, with all
the intermediate lanes and buildings.

Ward 3:
The third ward shall include the south side of Rotten Row, the east
side of the High Street from said Row, including Queensberry Square,
to the north side of McGeorge's Close, and from thence, in a nearly
straight line west-ward, past the Tradeshall and cross down Grierson's
Close to Irish Street, including the north side of said close, and also
including the whole of the High Street, from the north side of Grierson's
Close to the head of Friars Vennel, the New Fleshmarket Street or East
Barnraws (Queensberry Street), from Townhead Street to Lochmabengate
(English Street) on both side and both sides of King Street, with all the
intermediate lanes and buildings.

Ward 4:

The fourth ward shall comprehend the whole of Bank Vennel on both sides, also that part of west Barnraws or Irish Street, from the said Friars Vennel to Assembly Street, on both sides and part of the sands from said Vennel to Assembly Street, the east corner of Queensberry Square, or south side of McGeorge Close, and the whole line of the street in intermediate lanes and buildings from thence to the corner of Lochmabengate Street, thence across that street and including the Kings Arms, Custom House, Close and tenements, and Johnstone's Shop and tenements, and from thence, including Assembly Street on both sides; this ward shall also comprehend the High Street, with all the intermediate lanes and buildings from Grierson's Close, to the head of Assembly Street and Mid Rows, including the whole building between Tradeshall and the old Coffee House, and the Cross and the old Court House buildings.

Ward 5:

The fifth ward shall comprehend the whole of Lochmabengate Street on both sides and the whole of Queen's Street on both sides, and the whole of Shakespeare's Street from Lochmabengate Street to Nith Place on both sides, also the Milnhole on both sides from Shakespeare's Street to the Kirkgate Street and all the intermediate lanes and buildings.

Ward 6:

The sixth ward shall commence at the end of Johnstone the bookseller's shop, on the one side, and the south side of Assembly Street on the other, and shall comprehend the High Street, and all the intermediate lanes and buildings, from these points on both sides to the Milnburn on the east side and to Mrs. Sweetman's corner of Irish Street, on the other, also the whole of Irish Street from Assembly Street to the said corner on both sides, also the north side of Nith Street, and round the Sands to Assembly Street, the whole of Kirkgate Street on both sides, beginning at the Milnburn on the east side and including the south side of Nith Street on the other, and the whole intermediate lanes and buildings, also the whole property on the east side of the Dock.

And let it be further enacted that the Provost and three Baillies, and the Deacon Convener of the Trades of the said town of Dumfries, for the time being, and two commissioners for each of the said six wards, elected in manner herein after mentioned, shall be, and are hereby appointed Commissioners for assessing, levying and applying the monies, hereinafter directed to be raised for the purpose aforesaid, for naming and appointing a Clerk, Collector, Servants, Master of Police, Superintendents of Fire Engine, Watchmen, Firemen and other officers for fixing their salaries, for regulating the manner of cleansing, lighting, paving, watching, guarding, and patrolling the streets, for establishing rules and regulations for the direction and government of the said

Clerk, Collector and other officers aforesaid, and for executing the other matters specified in this Act and committed to their charge......"

On 17th June 1811 the burgh council also notified the public of an election under terms of the new Act:

"NOTICE

IS HEREBY given, that Friday the 28th day of JUNE current, is fixed for the purpose of electing Commissioners for the several Wards; and that Boxes will be put up at the places after-mentioned, so that all concerned may have access to deposit their voted:

WARD 1ST. box to placed at the door of Mr. Stott the glass grinder
WARD 2ND. box to be placed at the front of Conveynor McNaught's house, Friars Vennel
WARD 3RD. box to be placed at the shop door of Mr. John Hair, cloth merchant
WARD 4th. box to be place at the old Coffee House door)
WARD 5th. box to be placed at the corner of the house belonging to Mr. Coulthard, Saddler, Lochmabengate
WARD 6th. box to be place at the door of Mr. Hannah's house, cabinet maker, Nith Place.

Joseph Gass
Council Chambers, Dumfries
17th June 1811"

Chapter Two
THE SERGEANTS

Policing the burgh changed when, upon acceptance of the new Act, on 3rd July, 1811. The 'Act' adopted by the burgh also created a new 'police' offences:

> *"And if any person or persons shall obstruct, hinder or molest, any Watchman, or other officer, under this Act, every person so offending, shall forfeit and pay a sum not exceeding Forty Shillings sterling for each offence. And if any person or persons assault any Watchman, or other officer, employed in the performance of his duty under this Act, every person or persons shall, for every such offence, forfeit and pay a sum not exceeding five pounds sterling. And if any proprietor or possessor of a house or houses shall at any time lets by the year, or otherways, such houses or parts thereof, to vagrant, idle, and disorderly persons, or public and sturdy beggers, or suspicious persons, failing to have lawful occupations or employment, such proprietors or possessors shall, for every such offence, forfeit and pay a penalty not exceeding five pounds sterling."*

On 15th July that year the following appeared in the Dumfries Weekly Journal:

> *"POLICE OF DUMFRIES*
>
> *THE COMMISSIONERS under the new Police Act wish to engage a proper person for MASTER of POLICE; and, from the nature of the duties required to be performed, that would prefer a respectable Mechanic. They have also occasion for SIX WATCHMEN, who are at the same time, in case of necessity, to act as Firemen, and who must be active men, and of good character. Liberal encouragement will be given, and particulars may be learnt on application to Thomas Fraser, writer, Clerk to the Commissioners."*

Alexander Crombie, a stonemason, was appointed as Master of Police on a wage of £40 per annum. Mr. Crombie, like the previous superintendents of police, was not a policeman, but a council official, responsible for lighting, paving, cleaning and watching the burgh. Each of the six wards was to have a watchman sworn in as a constable and supervised by a burgh sergeant.

In each ward there was a box where the watchmen would start and finish his patrol or his 'perambulations' and he would likely rest or take cover during foul weather in his police box. There are also several references to the watchmen being dismissed for being found asleep or drunk in their box.

The council looked for their first sergeant of the guard to look after the watchmen of the town guard and appointed Samuel Gibson. Little else is known of Samuel Gibson other than he was to be a council servant, in various guises, for some time after this date. Two other watchmen appointed at the time were Charles Dargavel and John Millar. These watchmen were different from the burgh officers and only worked at night between 9pm and 4am.

On 13th August 1811, Sergeant Gibson requested that the watchmen be given waistcoats and the police commissioners agreed to this, giving them cutlasses as well. The commissioners also established a guardhouse and lock up on the north side of the Midsteeple for people apprehended by the guard during the night. This police office stood approximately where the current Timpson' Shoe Repair shop stands today. Prior to this the burgh officers just kept their custodies in the cell in the Midsteeple or at the prison until they appeared before the magistrates the following morning. The cell at the Midsteeple, also called the 'Saut Box', was at the base of the clock tower on the east side of the building.

At this meeting Walter Newall was appointed as superintendent of the new burgh fire engine and John Livingstone was appointed as a watchman.

On 26th November 1811 the commissioners employed four 'scavengers' to sweep the street and keep them clean. They also appointed Stewart Dunbar, a stonemason, James Bruce, a gardener and James Campbell, a pensioner as watchmen. There was no national state pension and no compulsory retirement age, so people just kept on working until they were so old or infirm that they couldn't carry on: Campbell was likely a former soldier with a small pension.

During its inaugural year the Dumfries Burgh Police consisted of the earliest recorded full time police officers in the region:

> Sergeant Samuel Gibson
> Constable Charles Dargavel,
> Constable John Millar
> Constable Stewart Dunbar,
> Constable James Bruce,
> Constable James Campbell and
> Constable John Livingstone

In February 1812 Charles Dargavel and John Millar were reported to the commissioners by Sergeant Gibson for apparently giving up their post.

The commissioners ordered that they be apprehended and taken before the magistrates for punishment. Watchman James McKenzie was reported for sleeping on the job and reprimanded as it was a first offence. Likewise Watchman William Wilson was reported for being intoxicated and cautioned as to his future conduct.

At this meeting, Joseph Wilson, Peter Robertson and Thomas Carruthers were appointed as watchmen and sworn in as constables under the Police Act.

On 2nd July, 1812 Thomas Hayton, Thomas Cairns and Michael Brodie were all sworn in as watchmen while Sergeant Gibson was dismissed for improper conduct; he apparently insulted a lady. James Carruthers was appointed as sergeant in his place. At this meeting the commissioners under a petition also agreed to change the name of Lochmabengate to English Street.

On 16th July 1812 Samuel Gibson was re-appointed as a watchman and, at the same meeting, the commissioners agreed to change the name of Kirkgate to St Michael Street. James Welsh was appointed as a watchman, while Watchman Michael Brodie resigned and was replaced by William McKeand.

On 9th April 1813 Sergeant of the Guard, James Carruthers, resigned having been cautioned by the commissioners for not lending aid to a burgh officer who was struggling with a prisoner he had arrested under power of a warrant. Samuel Gibson, the first Sergeant of the Town Guard, was thereafter re-appointed as sergeant and James Kennan was appointed as a watchman as was Andrew Fraser just a month later.

At the Annual General Meeting of the Police commissioners on 25th July 1813, Alexander Crombie was re-confirmed as Superintendent of Police and Sergeant Gibson re-confirmed as Sergeant of the Town Guard.

The Dumfries and Galloway Courier reports on the 6th April 1813:

"On Saturday night, an attempt was made by some villains to break into the cellar and shop of Mr. John Brand, at the head of King Street here, but we are happy to say, they were frustrated in their diabolical design. They had, it is supposed, first proceeded to the cellar door, which they bored in thirteen places with a centre bit, making a hole of nearly an inch diameter, for the purpose of finding the bolt, but the door was so strongly secured that they could not effect their purpose. They then proceeded to a back or staircase door, which led into the shop, and bored a hole so directly onto the bar, that it may be pushed back and forward with the greatest ease. As no further attempt was made, it is believed they had been alarmed by some persons passing, which caused them to make off."

On 14th December 1813 Sergeant Gibson reported that the watchmen's greatcoat's were worn and in need of replacement and the commissioners agreed to have them replaced. It is unclear what the uniform of the Town Guard was although it is known that they were given a hat, a greatcoat, a waistcoat and a cutlass, there would also be a coloured ribbon or lace on the hat to identify them as town officials.

At a meeting on 4th July 1814 the police commissioners decreed that it was not allowable for a watchman to be the keeper of a public house. This rule still applies today as police legislation prevents a serving police officer from holding a liquor licence.

On 5th August 1814 James Kennan, William Sturgeon and James Welsh were suspended from duty for misconduct. The commissioners upon hearing the case decided that they should be reprimanded. It is not know what their misconduct was, but the two favourites of the time were sleeping on duty or being intoxicated either on or off duty.

On 27th September 1814 Sergeant Samuel Gibson was again dismissed, this time for being found asleep on duty by Commissioners Hayland and Riddick. The police commissioners agreed with their colleagues and Sam Gibson was out of work again. At the same meeting Robert Ross was appointed as a watchman and immediately promoted to Sergeant of the Guard. At the next meeting James Jackson, was dismissed for sleeping on the job; he was replaced by James Maxwell.

On 22nd December 1814 it was reported to the commissioners that the watchmen were spending too much time standing talking to people on their wards or beats. The commissioners dictated that the sergeant of the guards should ensure that the watchmen perambulate urgently about their wards and prevent crowds of persons from gathering upon the streets.

During the following meeting it was decided that more watchmen were needed and James Jackson, who had been dismissed a month or so earlier, was reinstated as a watchman. They also agreed that John Black a serving soldier should be employed when his commission with the artillery was complete.

On 7th February 1815 upon a report by Sergeant Ross, William McKeand was dismissed for repeatedly sleeping on duty and James Welsh was dismissed for being frequently intoxicated. John Black was also dismissed for being an Innkeeper. Samuel Gibson and John Black were reappointed as watchmen at the next meeting together with a new applicant, John Irving.

Devastation followed in the meeting of 15th March 1815 when finding themselves short of funds the commissioners decided that they could do without a superintendent of police and, that faithful servant Alexander Crombie, was given one months notice. To save money they also dismissed three watchmen, namely Thomas Cairns, James Jackson and Alexander Fraser. A short time later Alexander Crombie found himself charged and convicted of theft and sentenced to imprisonment. The commissioners decided that his wages should stop from the date of his conviction saving them paying his wages in lieu of his notice.

The weekly wages of the remaining watchmen was also reduced from 10 shillings and sixpence to eight shillings. In today's currency that was from 52 1/2 pence to forty pence. The commissioners also dictated that no watchman could employ a substitute unless through illness.

On 13th June 1816 the commissioners finally decided to permanently do away with the office of superintendent of police and co-joined it with the office of sergeant of the guard. Robert Ross was offered the job and accepted it at the same wages he had for being sergeant of the guard. He was, in effect, now looking after the street paving, the sanitation, the public lighting and supervising the watchmen for the same wage as he had when just supervising the watchmen. James Maxwell was appointed corporal of the guard and deputy to Robert Ross.

In September that year James Maxwell left the police and was appointed a burgh officer and James Thomson was appointed as Corporal of the Guard. Andrew Fraser was appointed as a watchman. The watchmen's nightly wage was increased to 1 shilling and sixpence per night.

On 6th December 1816 James Jackson was re-appointed as a watchman and the commissioners instructed the Sergeant to ensure that the watchmen assembled in the morning at the end of their tour of duty and reported to him all occurrences. He was in return to report all occurrences to the council chambers.

On 3rd January 1817 Samuel Gibson was appointed corporal of the guard in place of Corporal James Thomson who had died. Only a week later and Samuel Gibson was appointed as a burgh officer and John Edmonston was appointed as corporal of the guard. James Walkend was employed as a watchman.

In May 1817 Corporal Cairns was suspended for striking a prisoner. He was severely reprimanded. There being no previous report of his promotion to corporal and no other mention of Corporal John Edmonston, we can only presume that Edmonston had left and was replaced by Corporal Cairns.

On 16th June, 1817 the meeting heard a complaint against Mr. Coupland presently employed as the carter of the street dung and terminated his employment immediately and on 28th July that year Sergeant Robert Ross, was sent to instruct Neil McDowall, a scavenger, that he was dismissed for insolence to the commissioners.

On 17th June 1817 the Dumfries Weekly Journal reported as follows:

"A woman of the name of Isobel or Isobella Thomson, who was lately convicted of theft and housebreaking, was publicly whipped through the streets of this burgh, for returning from banishment, in pursuance of a sentence of the High Court of Justiciary."

On September 15th that year the commissioners invoked one of the powers of a royal burgh, namely, banishment from the burgh. Margaret Good was advised that she was permitted to remain in the town until Whit Sunday next as long as she and her landlord, John Clark, undertook not to beg in the street or become burdensome, however come next Whit Sunday she was to leave the town.

On 15th September 1817 Robert Ross resigned as sergeant of the police upon accepting a post as burgh officer. James Thomson was appointed sergeant in his place. About this time the commanding officer of the Dragoon Guards was requested to advise the dragoon privates not to ride their horses furiously in the street while the sergeant, James Thomson, was instructed to apprehend and take into custody and put into confinement all persons singing or calling speeches or ballads on the street after dark.

Constable James Jackson was summarily dismissed for going off duty between 2 and 3 in the morning and engaging in drinking whisky in a public house and causing a quarrel. John McDowall was thereafter appointed as his replacement.

On 4th September 1818 Sergeant James Thomson together with John McDowall, James Welsh and John Irving were called before the commissioners for poor conduct. Thomson, McDowall and Welsh were dismissed and Corporal Thomas Cairns was appointed temporary sergeant. At the next meeting McDowall was reinstated and Peter Grant was appointed as a watchman.

On 15th December 1818 the Dumfries Weekly Journal reported that:

"On Wednesday last, a man by the name of John Thomson, was whipped through the streets of Dumfries for having returned from banishment."

It was thereafter decided to appoint a captain of the guards and William Bryden was selected, while Thomas Cairns rank of temporary sergeant was continued. The commissioners also decided that the captain and his six police officers needed new greatcoats. Shortly thereafter Peter Grant was dismissed for drunkenness and swearing at the captain. William Smith was appointed as his replacement. William Sturgeon was stood down as a police officer owing to his great age and he was appointed a day officer with a remit to stand in for absent officers. James Wilson was appointed as a constable in his stead. A short time late William Smith resigned and Thomas Miller was appointed to replace him.

On 5th July 1819 William Bryden was re-selected as captain and sergeant of police. Thomas Cairns was re-selected as corporal and Andrew Chalmers was appointed as street dung carter. James Nelson was also dismissed for absenting himself from duty.

On 6th August 1819 Thomas Miller, a policeman, was brought before the commissioners charged with being in John Underwood's inn, drinking with a man and taking money from him. He denied the charge but upon being searched by the sergeant the money was found in his pocket. The commissioners dismissed him on the spot. William Fathers, late private of the Dragoon Guards, was appointed as a temporary replacement for Miller. Fathers was soon dismissed upon a report from the Captain that he had been found drunk on duty. John McNairn was appointed to replace him.

In December that year John Glendinning was appointed as a watchman and James Cairns and John Fairbairn were appointed as temporary watchmen at the same pay as the police officers. Cairns and Fairbairn were dismissed in March 1820 when the money to pay them was running low.

On 23rd June 1820 Captain Bryden was instructed to place an officer in each of the six wards of the burgh to prevent blackguards infesting the town. At the same meeting James Maxwell, a former police officer and now a burgh officer, was awarded 10 shillings and sixpence (52½ new pence) for frequently assisting the police of the burgh.

On 1st September, 1820 Fleshmarket Street was re-named Queensberry Street.

On 11th October 1820 the Dumfries Weekly Journal reported on a terrible murder at Dumfries Prison:

"REWARD OF TWENTY AND FIFTY GUINEAS

ATTROCIOUS MURDER

Yesterday, about one o' clock, THOMAS MORRIN, Turnkey of the Jail of Dumfries, was inhumanely MURDERED, by DAVID HAGGART, one of the prisoners, by striking him on the head with a large stone, put into a bag for the purpose, by which his skull was fractured, and he died about ten o' clock last night.

The said David Haggart, immediately after committing the Murder, escaped from the Jail. He is a native of Edinburgh, 22 years of age, and about five feet eight inches high, slender made, with fair hair, and dark eyes; wore a black coat and vest, drab pantaloons, a black handkerchief, white stockings and thin pumps; speaks quick; has a stoppage or hesitation in beginning to speak; and is well known about Edinburgh and Leith. It is believed he had about £5 in money when he escaped.

Whoever apprehends and lodges him in any of His Majesty's jails after this notice, will receive a REWARD from the Town of Dumfries of TWENTY GUINEAS, and a further REWARD from the County of FIFTY GUINEAS.

These rewards will be paid upon a Certificate from the Magistrates and Sheriff, that Haggart is safely lodged in jail.

Dumfries, 11th Oct. 1820"

On 17th October 1820 the Dumfries Weekly Journal reports:

"ATROCIOUS MURDER

On Tuesday last, about one o'clock, Thomas Morrin, the turnkey of the jail here, was most inhumanly murdered by David Haggart, one of the prisoners, which he effected in the following manner:- While two clergymen were in the cell with the condemned criminal, Morrin was called upon to let them out, and as he was going up for that purpose, and at the same time carrying the prisoner's dinner, Haggart, who had concealed himself in a closet in the staircase, as soon as the unfortunate man passed him, struck him with a large stone put into a bag, by which his skull was fractured, and he died the same evening. Haggart, having thus got possession of the key, immediately made his escape, and though unremitting search has ever since been made for him, no traces have yet been discovered. A reward of 70 Guineas (£105) has been offered for the apprehension of Haggart, and we trust, it will not be long before he is secured. The deceased was a very decent man, and has left a wife and family to deplore his fate. A subscription, we are happy to understand, has been set on foot for his distressed and disconsolate family, which, the shocking circumstances of the case, will be, we have no doubt, liberal as well as general."

On 24th October 1820 the Dumfries Weekly News commented on the development of the case against Haggart:

"We regret to state, that notwithstanding the most active and unremitting exertions continue to be employed to discover and apprehend David Haggart, the murderer of our late under jailor, the villain still remains at large. For the last two or three evenings the English coach, on its arrival, has been surrounded by crowds of people, anxious to hear of his apprehension. We still indulge the hope, that he

will not long escape detection. Much praise is due to the Magistracy for the zeal they have displayed in this melancholy business. We are happy to understand, that the subscription for the relief of the distressed widow and her family now amounts to a very handsome sum; a circumstance which does honour to the benevolent feelings of our fellow townsmen."

Haggart was later traced, tried and found guilty of murder at Edinburgh on 15th June 1821. He was hanged on 18th June 1821 and his body handed over the medical school for dissection.

On 8th October 1820 Edward McRory was hanged in the prison yard of Dumfries Prison. McRory, who was also known as McLory or McGrory was 31 and came from Ballybreck in Ireland. He was charged with assault and robbery at Carse of Slacks, Gatehouse of Fleet, where he attacked and robbed Hugh Gallagher of £5. He was tried and convicted at Dumfries.

His execution is recorded in the Dumfries Weekly News dated 24th October 1820:

"EXECUTION:

On Wednesday last, about three o'clock p.m. was executed here, Edward McLory, a native of Ireland, pursuant to his sentence, for the crimes of highway robbery and attempted murder, as formerly stated in out paper. The Magistrates, the Commissioners of Police, the Constables and the staff of the Militia, attended; and previous to the fatal drop being let down, the Rev. Dr Scott, minister of St. Michael's Church, gave a most impressive and affecting prayer, and a hymn was sung, which being joined in by the immense multitude assembled, had a very solemn and imposing effect. During his confinement, people of various persuasions humanely offered him every religious consolation in their power; the following account, however, we believe will be found correct:

Having, after his condemnation, professed himself Catholic, he was assiduously attended by the Rev. Mr. Carruthers, who found him at first very ignorant, seemingly of weak intellect, and altogether wild and extravagant in his ideas. He seemed, however, so far to profit by instructions, as to acquire some knowledge of the leading principles of Christianity, and of the awful alternative of eternal happiness or misery; he acknowledged his crime, the justness of his sentence, and expressed sentiments of contrition, resignation to his fate, and hopes of divine mercy.

When the hour of execution drew nigh, he appeared much agitated. After his fetters were knocked off, on seeing the executioner approach for the purpose of pinioning his arms, he was seized with a sudden paroxysm, and struck a sudden blow at him, which he instantly

*regretted asked pardon and promised to abstain from all future
resistance. He then went peaceably to the place of execution, knelt
down with Mr. Carruthers, and seemed to join fervently in prayer with
him. On ascending the scaffold, he attempted to harangue the crowd,
especially his countrymen, but his expressions were such an incoherent
rhapsody, as rendered it impossible clearly to comprehend him. Mr.
Carruthers endeavoured to soothe him, and persuade him to calm
his thoughts on God, and employ to better purpose his few remaining
moments. He complied, drew down his cap, dropped the handkerchief,
and was launched into eternity almost without a shrink or motion. He
was 31 years of age."*

On 2nd April 1821 Constable John McDowall was dismissed for fraudulently altering a receipt and sleeping on duty. He appealed to the commissioners but his appeal was turned down and Thomas Cairns, who was with him when the fraudulent act was committed, was reprimanded as the commissioners accepted that he wasn't good at writing and figures. John Fairbairn was appointed as a police officer in McDowall's place.

In September that year Constable Andrew Fraser was charged with theft, but after a hearing in front of the commissioners the charges were found to be not proven. James Nelson, meanwhile, was dismissed for insolence and Thomas Hayton was reprimanded for sleeping on duty. Thomas Gracie was appointed to replace Nelson.

On June 6th 1821 James Gordon, an Irishman, was publicly hanged at Dumfries Prison for the murder of a young pedlar, John Elliot. Gordon had met Elliot at a farm in Canonbie Parish where they spent the night. Gordon pretended to know a short cut across the hills to Moffat and induced Elliot to accompany him. Gordon then murdered Elliot near Upper Cassock, Eskdalemuir, by beating him about the head before rifling his belongings. Gordon's description was circulated, but no trace of him could be found.

Several months later a traveller at Nairn, Inverness, was leafing through an old copy of the Dumfries newspaper and read of the murder and the description of the man that the justices wanted for the crime. Upon looking up he found Gordon standing right in front of him. Gordon was accosted and held until the police arrived. Gordon was thereafter arrested and taken to Dumfries where he was tried, found guilty and sentenced to death.

The 'Journal' reporting on the execution commented:

*"What added unspeakable interest to the awful crisis, and gave
it, indeed, the character of wild and appalling sublimity, was the
remarkable circumstances, that the moment in which the prisoner took
his place on the drop was indicated by a vivid flash of lightening and a
tremendous burst of thunder".*

'The Police Act Page 30 & 31 it is enacted that the Master of Police and other officers appointed by the commissioners shall aid and assist the magistrates of the Town in apprehending and putting the laws in execution against Vagabonds, Vagrants, Idle and disorderly Persons, Public and Sturdy Beggars and other persons who follow no legal employment or occupation."

On 7th January 1822 it was decided to rebuild the guardhouse at the Midsteeple. The contract, which was priced at £20 was to extend the building, put in higher ceilings and make a cell in the basement.

On 21st May, 1822 Thomas Gracie resigned and was replaced by Albert Little, while at the meeting of 15th June 1822 the commissioners decided that the Sergeant William Bryden, could, when necessary, suspend the policemen and appoint others in their place until the commissioners could decide how to deal with the offending officers.

In August 1822 the following appeared as a Dumfries Weekly Journal report on the police court proceedings:

"JULY 1 – Charles King, a slater in Dumfries, was brought before the Magistrates, accused of wantonly striking a man upon the public street: the case was clearly proved, and he was sentenced to pay a fine of £1, or be imprisoned 14 days.

Same day, the said Charles King, was fined a further sum of 10s. 6d. sterling, for going into a public house and drinking to the value of 2s. 6 pennies: and breaking several articles amounting to 2s. 6d: more and of which he refused to pay, and for abusing the landlord. The Magistrates also discerned him to pay the 5s. In addition to the fine, or eight days imprisonment – Having paid both fines, he was after a suitable admonition with regard to his future conduct, discharged.

JULY 8 – Agnes Glen and Mary McIvor, women of bad fame, were sentenced to eight days imprisonment, for being continually on the streets at night, annoying and disturbing the peaceable inhabitants.

Same day, Andrew Henderson, cooper, and Joseph McGregor, tinsmith, were sentenced to thirty days confinement in jail, for a most aggravated assault committed upon two decent servant girls in the outskirts of the town, upon the evening of Sunday last. – Two others, art and part in the disgraceful affair, have absconded.

JULY 4 – John Johnstone, flesher, was sentenced to 14 days imprisonment, for striking a woman at the door of her own house.

Same day, Samuel McNairne, innkeeper, William McCaa, weaver, and Ivor Burgess, carter, all residing in Dumfries, were sentenced to thirty days imprisonment, for assaulting and striking the Sergeant of Police and Burgh Officer and obstructing them whilst in the execution of their duty."

On 6th September, 1822, Sergeant Bryden reported that Robert Selkirk, a Flesher (butcher) of Buccleuch Street had placed meats on a stand outside his premises and refused to remove it. The commissioners instructed the Sergeant that should this occur again he was to seize the meat and the stand and bring the transgressors before the magistrates.

On 7th February 1823 it is reported that Robert Little was injured on duty and unable to attend his duty that night, although there is no description of the injury or how it happened. The commissioners decided that the Sergeant should find a replacement for Little and agreed to continue to pay his salary in the meantime.

In April, 1823 the Sergeant was given a new hat with a silver band to denote his authority. At the same meeting the commissioners were advised of three officers being found drunk on duty. After deliberation they found all three guilty and fined them ten shillings (50p) each.

On 14th May 1823 Irish immigrant John McKana or McKena aged 39 years a stone dyker of Quaas near Lockerbie, his wife Hannah Black or McKana, Joseph Richardson a joint tenant of Gilmour Banks, Lochmaben and William Richardson a 32 year old from Maxwellsbraehead, Lochmaben were tried at Dumfries for the forgery and uttering of banknotes from the Ship Bank of Glasgow. John McKana and Joseph Richardson were convicted of the crime and sentenced to be hanged at Dumfries Prison.

"EXECUTION.

A full and particular account of the Execution and behaviour of JOHN M'KANA, alias M'KENA, and JOSEPH RICHARDSON, for the crime of uttering as genuine false and forged notes, who were EXECUTED at Dumfries, on Wednesday the 14th day of May, 1823.

The above persons, as also William Richardson, brother to the said Joseph, were all three tried at Dumfries, and condemned to death on Wednesday the 9th day of April last, by the Right Honourable Lord Meadowbank; but since which, on Thursday the 1st instant, the Magistrates received a letter from the Right Honourable Robert Peel, Secretary of State for the Home Department, stating that his Majesty had been graciously pleased to grant a reprieve in favour of William Richardson, the eldest of the two unfortunate brothers, commuting his punishment to banishment for life. The intelligence was communicated to him by the Provost, (in presence of the different Ministers of the town), and he received the glad tidings with becoming thankfulness, and expressed his gratitude to those individuals who had so earnestly and successfully interested themselves in his behalf. His brother Joseph continued to the last to be deeply affected by the awful fate that awaited him, and diligently attended to the instructions of those Rev. Gentlemen who daily visited him. It is also consolatory to learn, that the conduct of M'Kana, the Irishman, was in every respect most exemplary for his situation, tho' professing the Roman Catholic creed. He was far from being bigoted; but on the contrary, was most anxious to receive the advice and assistance of the Clergymen of every denomination, all of whom express themselves much satisfied with the state of his mind, and the resignation which he manifested. He was by no means ignorant of religious matters, indeed, his general knowledge, makes it the more to be lamented, that he had not applied his talents to some honest purpose. During the trial, which was long and tedious, it appeared that M'Kana, and Hannah Black, his wife, had 72, and Joseph Richardson 163 forged notes, knowingly in their possession, without lawful excuse, at their dwelling places, Lockerbymuir and Gilmourbank. The Richardsons appear to be about from 35 to 40 years of age, and M'Kana about 50. While his Lordship was passing sentence, the panel Joseph Richardson, fainted. During their long confinement, every indulgence has been granted them, as far as the nature of their unfortunate situation would admit; and the prayers of the different congregations has not been omitted in their behalf; and these unfortunate men have conducted themselves both before and since their trial with becoming propriety.

A new drop has been erected for the occasion, and so rare it is for two to be executed here at same time, that it has but once occurred for more than sixty years, and that was the two brothers for housebreaking, and it is to be hoped it will be much longer before such an occurrence takes place again, as moral and religious instruction is by no means wanting in this part of the country, when listened to. There were an immense crowd assembled to witness their melancholy exit; the number cannot be estimated at less than 10,000. From the Post-Office to the New Bridge was one dense and unbroken mass; every window and lamp-post was literally crowded. About a quarter before three, they ascended the fatal steps.

After the prisoners had been seated, a very impressive prayer was delivered by Dr Scott, to which they seemed to listen with apparent resignation and reverence. After some preliminary circumstances were got over, linen caps were then drawn over their features, by which they were wholly concealed; and after the rope was adjusted, a solemn silence prevailed. The fatal signals were given, and in a few moments all was over! Their straggles were short. After their bodies were cut down, and incoffined, they were delivered to their friends for interment. To *prevent such crimes and such rigid punishment as is by law awarded to offenders, let such a full example as is intended be the means of preventing and deterring others from entailing misery and disgrace on themselves and posterity."*

Provost Thomson intimated that each of the councillors should take it in turn to be superintendent of police in a weekly rotation. This was agreed and Captain McDowall, a councilor carried out the first duty. He reported back to the commissioners on 7th September 1823 advising that only the sergeant had a lamp or lantern and that only two of the policemen had a rattle. He also complained of a very offensive smell in the watch house due to a lack of ventilation. He further stated that the sergeant and his officers were all on duty when he carried out his inspection and he observed that they had all behaved themselves properly.

At this meeting Sergeant Bryden reported that Andrew Fraser, a watchman, had taken ill and was unfit for duty. He was instructed to recruit a replacement and Fraser was awarded one shilling (5p) per day. It is later reported that on 5th March 1824 (six months later) Fraser was still off ill and his wages were stopped.

On 12th August 1823 the following was reported in the Glasgow press:

"A gentleman in Edinburgh, on Friday last, sent his servant to the bank with a check for £50. The fellow absconded with the money. The criminal officers in Glasgow heard of the theft, and were on the alert. About one o'clock on Sunday morning they found the object of their pursuit in bed in a house in Cowcaddens. Forty pounds of the money were found in his pocket. When ordered to rise and follow the officers, "sure", says Pat, "you won't take me away till I spake with a friend that's but just now in a neighbour's house". A messenger was instantly dispatched for the friend; but instead of one friend, about forty arrived, who rescued the fellow out of the hands of the officers."

On 7th September Watchmen Glendinning, Little and Fairbairn (who had been fined ten shillings each back in April for being drunk) all apologised and appealed to the commissioners for a reduction in their fines. The commissioners were unmoved by the appeal and refused to reduce the fines.

On 2nd December 1823 Thomas Hayton was found drunk on duty and refused to assist in apprehending a man rioting in the street. Hayton was fined ten shillings.

On 19th December John Fairbairn was reported for being drunk on duty (his second offence in a short period) and Thomas Cairns was found guilty of neglect of duty. The commissioners dismissed them and they were later replaced by John Gair and John Ball. Andrew Fraser was no longer fit to return to duty and was replaced by Thomas Graham.

In March 1824 the sergeant was awarded 19 shillings and six pence as he had been off sick and had to pay for a replacement, the commissioners remunerated him for his trouble.

On 2nd April 1824 the commissioners produced 200 copies of a document of the regulations of police officers and each of the commissioners and the Police Officers were given a copy. From that point on all policemen were required to produce this copy of the regulations by any inhabitant who required it. While not quite a warrant card it is the first reference to policemen carrying a letter of authority other than a baton of office or a coloured lace on their hats.

In June 1824 a Captain Baylay complained about the conduct of Sergeant Bryden of the watch. The commissioners heard the complaint and decided that Sergeant Bryden had acted in accordance with his instructions when he apprehended the captain for being noisy and creating a disturbance, the complaint was dismissed.

On 4th March 1825 Sergeant Bryden was suspended and while he was allowed to remain in post his name was put into the 'Book of Delinquency' by the magistrates. At the same time John Bell, who had been injured while on duty was allowed six days wages while he had been unfit for duty.

On second of May 1825 John Glendinning was dismissed by the magistrates and John Bell reprimanded. George Brown of Lochvale was appointed in place of Glendinning.

The cost of running the council was forever at the forefront of the council meetings and the following is some costs heading from 30th May 1825.

> "Watchmen, fire monies and new greatcoats: £ 215:11:07
> Scavengers: (Street Cleaners) £ 138:17:04
> Street Repairs: £ 221:09:03
> Lamps: (Oil Lamps maintenance and repair) £ 47:18:00
> Salaries: (Council Staff) £ 53:03:00
> Arrears (Monies owed to Council) £ 189:10:11
> Misc. Charges:
> (Rents, printing, interest on loans etc.) £ 1009:13:08"

On 4th July 1825 a complaint was lodged against Sergeant Bryden and Thomas Hayton and having been found guilty by the magistrates, they were both dismissed immediately. Thomas Graham was appointed sergeant on a salary of £30 per annum. At the same meeting John Brand a council clerk and tax collector was appointed as superintendent of police, while on 5th August the commissioners also appointed John Crosbie, a shoemaker of Maxwelltown and John Charters, a pensioner, as officers of Police.

On 22nd September 1825 John Gair was dismissed, 'on account of his former faults'. Samuel Carruthers was appointed in his place.

On 31ˢᵗ October 1825 the Sheriff Court sat at Dumfries:

"SHERIFF COURT OF DUMFRIES

A criminal court was held by Sir Thomas Kirkpatrick, Bart., Sheriff Depute of the county, for the trial of two delinquents by jury.

The first was that of Nathanial Dunscath or Dunscaith, carter in Brewery Street of Dumfries, accused of having on the 11th day of May last, assaulted James Maxwell, burgh officer in Dumfries, while in the execution of personal diligence against the panel, within the house of William Currie, innkeeper on Sands of Dumfries and also in the Friars Vennel, and of striking him several severe blows. And of again assaulting the said James Maxwell, when of new endeavouring to execute the said personal diligence on the 12th of may last, at the crossing of the Friars Vennel and Brewery Street, by striking him a severe blow with the butt end of a whip, and aiming a blow at the belly of one of his assistants with a large knife, which he had previously drawn from his pocket: and when Maxwell endeavoured to seize the knife, of inflicting two severe cuts on his left hand with it; and on being rescued from said James Maxwell and assistants, by the aid of some evil disposed bystanders, of instantly flying at, and striking the said James Maxwell, several severe blows on the face, and knocking his head against the wall of the street, whereby, he was disabled from attempting to put the said warrant into execution.

The panel pled guilty to the assault on 12th May, but not guilty to the one on the 11th, nor the aggravation of committing it with a knife, or other lethal instrument: on which, the jury, having returned a verdict of finding him guilty in terms of his own confession, the sheriff, after a suitable admonition, sentenced him to be imprisoned in the tollbooth of Dumfries for one calendar month.

The other case was that of Janet Copland, daughter of James Copland, tenant of Fountainbleau, in the parish of Dumfries, accused of having on 20th September last, attacked and assaulted Mrs. Mary Mathews or Allan, wife of John Allan of Fountainbleau, and of striking her a severe blow on the back part of the head, with a large stone, thrown by the panel at her when about to enter the door of her own house, whereby, she was cut to the bone and lost a great quantity of blood. This case went to trial and a number of witnesses were examined on both sides, and although it was established for the prosecution that the stone had been thrown by the panel;, as charged in the indictment, yet it was proved on the other hand, that the panel had received very gross verbal provocation before having recourse to such a weighty and leveling argument. The jury were addressed by Mr. Young, the Fiscal, and by Mr. Fraser for the panel; after which the case was summed up by the judge. The jury, having retired, returned with a verdict finding the panel guilty, by a plurality of voices, but recommending her to the leniency of the Court on account of her previous good character, and the verbal provocation she had received in the course of the affray, before the stone was thrown.

In pronouncing sentence, the judge said he was always willing to listen to the recommendations of a jury, and he was happy that in the present case it would be in his power to dispense with inflicting that punishment upon the female at the bar that is usually awarded in cases of assault, namely that of imprisonment; although in duty he was bound to inflict some punishment on all persons convicted before him in similar circumstances, yet he could not avoid taking that opportunity of stating, in the hearing of the female witness who had been assaulted, that he hoped this trial would have an equally beneficial effect on her temper and conduct, as of those of the person of the accused, as it was in evidence that the witness had used very provoking and initiating language to the panel on the occasion alluded to.

Janet Copland was then sentenced to pay a fine of three guineas, and dismissed."

On 2nd December 1825 John Crosbie was dismissed for being drunk on duty and he was replaced by John McNeil.

On the 18th October, 1826, James McManus was executed at Dumfries for assault and robbery of farmer, Andrew Smail of Beckton, Dryfesdale. The attack occurred on the Dumfries to Lockerbie Road. Smail was en route home when he was attacked by three men.

McManus, Platt and Flynn were charged with:

"Having on 5th August last, on the public road from Dumfries by Lochmaben to Lockerbie, at a part of the road near the farm of Beckton, in the parish of Dryesdale, occupied by Andrew Smaill, farmer, attacked and assaulted Mr. Smaill, and struck him a blow upon the head, thrown him down, and threatened to run him through with a knife if he made the least resistance; and robbed him of a note of the Carlisle Commercial Bank, dated Carlisle, 19th November, 1825, No, J.670, for one guinea, eighteen shillings in silver, a knife, a comb, and having tore and carried away the pocket of his waistcoat, containing a variety of accounts and other documents."

After the trail the 'Journal' reported:

"JAMES McMANUS (alias James Coyle, aged 17 years), ROBERT PLATT, and JAMES FLYNN were brought up to receive sentence. (Following a trial that started on 18th September 1826)

Lord Alloway said that in this case the law pointed out their duty. From the verdict, Platt and Flynn must be assoilzied and dismissed from the bar, but no alternative was left with regard to McManus but pronouncing the last sentence of the law, and proposed that the panel be executed at Dumfries on Wednesday the 18th October next.

Lord McKenzie after saying a few words to the prisoners Platt and Flynn and advising them to take warning by the very narrow escape they had made from the gallows, put on the fatal hat, and addressed himself to McManus, to whom he said he had a much more painful duty to perform that to his companions. He had been convicted on the clearest evidence of having been guilty of the crime of Robbery on the King's highway, a crime which from the remotest period of Scottish jurisprudence had been visited and properly visited with the punishment of death. It was true that the jury had recommended him to mercy, and that recommendation would be transmitted in the only quarter from which mercy could be sought, with that respect that was at all times due to the verdict of a respectable and intelligent jury; but he implored the prisoner to trust to that recommendation; for notwithstanding of it, the advisers of the foundation of mercy might find themselves compelled in the discharge of their sacred duty to consult the welfare of the community, and to decline stretching the Royal Prerogative to objects whom they might consider undeserving of mercy. Many had suffered death notwithstanding of such recommendations and he must therefore beseech the prisoner to spend the few days allotted to him in this world, in seeking the mercy from the great Judge before whose tribunal he must soon appear, and in this he had no doubt he would be assisted by the ministers of religion of the place.

Sentence was then pronounced acquitting Platt and Flynn and sentencing McManus to be EXECUTED at Dumfries on Wednesday the 18th October next, between the hours of two and four in the afternoon.

During the address McManus stood with uplifted hands; his eyes were suffused with tears and on the judge reading the sentence, he uttered a few convulsive sighs of despair, shaked hands with his fellow prisoners, and was taken from the court under the most agonised feelings. Before leaving the dock, he thanked his counsel, Mr Ferguson, for his assistance during the trial."

On 24th March 1826 the Clerk to the commissioners recorded:

"The Regulations for the Superintendent of Police as Signed by the Minute.

'That the Superintendent be appointed annually by the commissioners of Police: to be under their direction and that the yearly salary shall be fixed by them at the annual meeting when the office bearers are appointed.

That the Superintendent may be removed from office at the pleasure of the commissioners of Police.

That the Superintendent shall see all resolutions of the commissioners of Police at their meetings and the instructions given strictly carried out into execution.

That all the officers of Police shall be under the immediate charge of the Superintendent and he shall see that they discharge their duty accordingly to the printed regulations and he shall give them such instruction as the commissioners of Police may from time to time consider proper.

That he shall occasionally inspect the different Wards of the town at night to be satisfied that the officers are at their post.

That he shall have vigilant eye over the streets to prevent obstructions and nuisances of any kind remaining thereon after due notice being given to remove the same and that not being attended to he shall cause the offender to be apprehended and taken before a Magistrate to be fined according to law

That no persons taken up by the officers during the night can be liberated unless by a satisfactory security being lodged with the Superintendent that the prisoner may be produced to answer to the charge against him before a Magistrate in the morning.

That the Superintendent may suspend any officer for any fault or neglect of duty until the complaint is brought before the first meeting of the Police.

That at each monthly meeting of Police he shall make a report of the officers of the police, the conduct of the officers and the general order and tranquility of the town.

That all complaints by the inhabitants, as the masters of police, shall be lodged with the Superintendent who will duly attend to such as he

can receive himself and such as he cannot he will lay before the first
meeting of Police or in an urgent case he will without delay he will
apply for a requisition and call a special meeting in due form as the case
may be answered by the Commissioners."

On 23rd May 1826 it was business as usual and Sergeant Graham was suspended by the new superintendent for being drunk on duty. After examination by the magistrates the sergeant was re-instated to his post but only on the understanding that:

"'.....he shall be more guarded in the future."

On 1st December 1826 John Charters was suspended by the superintendent. He then moved his furniture out of his house and left Dumfries. The commissioners accordingly dismissed him and appointed Archibald Duncan in his place.

A more serious event occurred on 10th February 1827 when Watchman John Bell was suspended and brought before the magistrates charged that he and his family had purchased stolen wool from apprentices who were employed at premises belonging to Convener Lockup. After a hearing where Bell intimated his innocence, but admitted that his wife and family had occasion to purchase wool from Mr. Lockup, he was dismissed. David Thomson was appointed in place of Bell.

The same meeting the superintendent reported that he had suspended George Brown for threatening to strike the superintendent. Brown appeared personally, admitted his guilt and proffered a sincere apology for his conduct to the superintendent and the commissioners. The commissioners accepted the apology, admonished Brown and re-instated him to his post.

On 19th September 1826 the Dumfries Weekly Journal reported when gas lighting was erected in the town:

"DUMFRIES

A new light has been introduced into Dumfries. The people who formally walked in darkness, and stumbled as they went, have discovered the badness of their ways, and rectified them accordingly. In short, Dumfries has been lighted with gas. We rejoice to hear the spread of intelligence, but the spread of light rejoices us still more. We have some doubts of the Hamiltonian System, but Gordon's portable lamps impart to us the most unalloyed satisfaction. The same feeling seems to be universal at Dumfries. On the 1st of September the gas was introduced, and the effect it produced is incredible. There were public dinners and public rejoicings of all sorts. Several respectable individuals went mad. The whole population for a hundred miles around, came into the town to see what was to be seen....."

On 2nd April 1827 the clerk to the commissioners of police was instructed to look for suitable premises to act as a lock up for females. There is no prior reference to a separate lock up facility, but it must have been mooted during conversation at a previous meeting.

On 1st June 1827 the superintendent acted again and suspended Archibald McDonald and John McNeil for being drunk. Both were severely reprimanded and re-instated to duty. Meanwhile Robert Little resigned and James Kirkpatrick was appointed to replace him.

On 3rd August Sergeant Graham was suspended and charged with being drunk. The commissioners reproved him, gave him his last and final warning and re-instated him to duty.

On the 27th March 1828 the Dumfries Burgh Police consisted of:

> *Sergeant Thomas Graham*
> *1st Ward (Townhead, Academy St and Buccleuch St):*
> *Constable Samuel Carruthers*
>
> *2nd Ward (Whitesands and Brewery St):*
> *Constable James Kirkpatrick*
>
> *3rd Ward (High St, Queensberry Sq and Friars Vennel):*
> *Constable David Thomson*
>
> *4th Ward (High St, Fleshmarket St and Bank St):*
> *Constable Joseph Dobie*
>
> *5th Ward (English St, Queen St and Shakespeare St):*
> *Constable George Brown*
>
> *6th Ward (High St, Irish St, Nith Place and Dock Head):*
> *Constable James Dickson.*

On 30th September 1828 Constable Samuel Carruthers was in court giving evidence against Agnes or Nancy Black.

Agnes Black had been charged with the theft of a printed gown, a black shawl and two handkerchiefs from John Aikman, a weaver who resided in St Michael Street. His evidence was reported in the local paper:

> *"Samuel Carruthers, police officer, knows the panel, and has known her by character for two years by habit and repute a thief. She is known in the Police Office under character. Cross examined – knows her chiefly by what people say of her character as habit and repute a thief, and from her being banished the county.*
>
> *The jury were addressed by Mr. Allison, Advocate Depute, and by Mr. C Ferguson, for the panel; and the case was summed up by Lord Gillies, when the jury unanimously returned a verdict of Guilty, and she was sentenced to transportation for fourteen years."*

On 12th December 1828 Sergeant Graham was caught drinking yet again and suspended by the superintendent. The commissioners found him guilty and he was advised that if there was a re-occurrence he would be dismissed.

In 1829 Sir Robert Peel, Home Secretary, introduced the Bill that was to result in the establishment of the Metropolitan Police in the nation's capital and radically change policing practices across the country forever.

"The Metropolitan Police Act 1829 Chapter 44 10 Geo 4

An Act for improving the Police in and near the Metropolis.
[19th June 1829]

Whereas offences against property have of late increased in and near the metropolis; and the local establishments of nightly watch and nightly police have been found inadequate to the prevention and detection of crime, by reason of the frequent unfitness of the individuals employed, the insufficiency of their number, the limited sphere of their authority, and their want of connection and co-operation with each other: And whereas it is expedient to substitute a new and more efficient system of police in lieu of such establishments of nightly watch and nightly police, within the limits herein-after mentioned, and to constitute an office of police, which, acting under the immediate authority of one of his Majesty's principal secretaries of state, shall direct and control the whole of such new system of police within those limits."

On 6th February 1829 William Hare, one of the infamous Edinburgh murderers and body snatchers, Burke and Hare, passed through Dumfries on his way back to Ireland:

"Burke and Hare - The Body Snatchers

One of the most peculiar events to happen in Dumfries was the town's greatest riot which took place on 6th February 1829. The crimes of the Edinburgh "body snatchers" Burke and Hare who had strangled their victims and sold them to doctors for dissection had terrified all of Scotland. Burke was tried and executed but Hare, an Irishman, turned King's Evidence to save himself. He was granted free passage to Ireland and on his way to Portpatrick his coach stopped in Dumfries.

Word got around the town and immediately a huge angry mob, many thousands strong, assembled outside the King's Arms Hotel (now Boots Chemist shop in the High Street) where Hare was lodged while waiting for his coach to leave. Some of the mob burst into the hotel intent on killing him but he was taken to a small top room, for his own safety.

The coach was due to leave at 11am but Hare did not get on it. It drew out of the inn yard and struggled to the head of Buccleuch Street where it was stopped and searched. The mob immediately surged back to the King's Arms. Oddly enough during the afternoon a number of people were allowed to visit him. One woman nearly strangled him while the police were thinking of a method to get him out. If he had remained in the King's Arms until nightfall the mob would certainly have burst in and killed him. At 3pm a chaise and pair were brought to the hotel and a trunk was loaded as if he were about to leave. This was a decoy and the mob followed if half way round the town. Hare, however, had jumped out of a rear window and was bundled into another carriage at the rear of the hotel. The plan was to get him safely into the prison in Buccleuch Street. Some of the mob realised what was happening and set off in pursuit. He just made it to the prison. The mob was furious at being cheated and were about to burn down the door when a hundred special constables arrived to reinforce the police and militia.

By midnight, however, most of the mob had melted away and by 1am there were none left. Hare was woken from his sleep in the early hours and conveyed on his way. Everyone in Galloway knew he was coming and so instead he was set on the Annan road to England. Six months later his sister came to the hotel to collect some of his clothes which had been left behind in the confusion. They were pointed out to her, still lying in a corner of the top room - no one would touch them."

On 13th February 1829 George Brown and James Kirkpatrick were suspended and reported for being drunk on duty. Brown was warned, but kept his job, while Kirkpatrick was dismissed. David Nish was appointed to replace him.

On 6th March, 1829 Joseph Dobie resigned and was replaced by John Hunter and a short time later David Nish was dismissed for being drunk and replaced by James Nelson.

In mid December 1829 Sergeant Graham was again in trouble for drinking. He was suspended by the superintendent and after a hearing before the commissioners and a report from a special committee was drawn together to look at the evidence, he was dismissed. William Dickson was appointed sergeant in his place.

On 12th March 1830 following a motion by Provost John Fraser the council agreed to introduce gas lighting to the council chambers. £3 per annum was set aside for costs.

Sergeant Dickson suspended James Nelson for being found in a state of intoxication. Nelson admitted this to the commissioners and was dismissed. A more serious allegation was made against David Thomson. The cellar of W. James Bendall in Friars Vennel was entered about four in the morning and it was suspected that Constable David Thomson was involved in the crime. He was later found to be completely innocent and reinstated to his post.

Mr. Brand, the Superintendent of Police and tax collector tendered his resignation. He had kept poor health for some time and found the strain of both roles beyond him. He offered to stay on until a suitable replacement could be found, but also asked the council to let him keep his job as tax collector. The council obviously thought well of Mr. Brand as they let him retain the role of tax collector, but asked him to retain the post of superintendent of police and do the best he could until a replacement could be found.

In 1830 the council moved from their home at the Tollbooth in High Street and took residence within the Midsteeple. The Midsteeple had been build in 1701 as a courthouse, a jail, the town clerks chambers and council chambers, it had also been used as an arsenal for the town and also let out for other purposes.

On 19th March 1830 James Kirkpatrick, John Bell and Joseph Dunn were all appointed as constables.

A new hat with a band was ordered for the sergeant. The sergeant's uniform is described as a black coat with a red collar and a hat with a red or silver band.

On 5th July 1830 the commissioners were as good as their word when they appointed John Brand as tax collector together with John Gibson, both men to act as joint clerks. William Dickson was re-appointed as sergeant and Constable Samuel Carruthers was promoted to corporal.

Councillor Alexander McPherson was appointed as superintendent of the fire engine with a remuneration of 3 guineas per annum. Robert Walker was appointed as scavenger and John Steel appointed as dung carter.

David Thomson was found drunk on duty; he insulted Councillor McPherson and was suspended from duty. Meanwhile the commissioners discovered that Sergeant Dickson had applied for the post of sheriff officer and wrote to the sheriff of his exemplary service to the town. Dickson resigned his position a short time later when he was appointed as a sheriff officer. Thomas Black was thereafter appointed sergeant.

On 3rd January 1831 David Thomson was dismissed and John Walker appointed in his place.

On 1st July 1831, the Burgh police consisted of:

Superintendent John Bland
Sergeant Thomas Black

Corporal Samuel Carruthers
Constable James Kirkpatrick,
Constable John Bell,
Constable Joseph Dunn,
Constable George Brown and
Constable John Weems (or Wemys)

On 27th December 1831 the 'Journal' reported:

"ESCAPE FROM JAIL.

*On the evening of Friday last William Beattie, who had been
incarcerated in the jail of this town about a week before on a sentence
for trespass, made his escape in a manner that is not properly
ascertained. We may, however, mention, that the prisoners though
usually locked in at 4 o'clock in the afternoon are allowed ten minutes
respite about 8, and it is supposed that some of his companions had
found the means of concerting with him to throw a ladder of rope over
the wall at that time, by which, under the darkness of night he might
ascend and escape unnoticed. He has not yet, we understand, been
again apprehended."*

In 1832 the Europe wide cholera epidemic hit Dumfries. On 25th September,
1832 signs were put up by the magistrates, board of health and commissioners
of Police,

*"...earnestly entreating the Inhabitants collectively, and individually,
to lend their prompt assistance in instantly WATERING, WASHING
and CLEANSING the STREETS and LANES in those parts of the town
situated in their respective immediate neighbourhoods, and to repeat
the same operation daily. Hot lime will be furnished, by applying to the
commissioners of Police of the respective Wards."*

The memorial in St Michael's Church yard given the number of deaths as 420
souls, but it was later estimated by the number of coffins procured during this
period that approximately 900 people died in Dumfries directly or indirectly
due to this epidemic.

Along the west wall of St Michael's Cemetery lie the graves of those men,
women and children who succumbed to cholera and to mark their demise a
cenotaph was raised in memory:

*"IN THIS CEMETERY AND CHIEFLY WITHIN THIS ENCLOSURE,
LIE THE MORTAL REMAINS OF MORE THAN 420 INHABITANTS
OF DUMFRIES, WHO WERE SUDDENLY SWEPT AWAY BY
THE MEMORABLE INVASION OF ASIATIC CHOLERA, A.D.
MDCCCXXX11.*

THAT TERRIFIC PESTILENCE ENTERED THE TOWN ON 15TH SEPTEMBER, AND REMAINED TILL 27TH NOVEMBER; DURING WHICH PERIOD IT SEIZED AT LEAST 900 INDIVIDUALS, OF WHOM 44 DIED IN ONE DAY, AND NO MORE THAN 415 WERE REPORTED AS RECOVERED. THAT THE BENEFIT OF THIS SOLEMN WARNING MIGHT NOT BE LOST TO POSTERITY, THIS MONUMENT WAS ERECTED, FROM COLLECTIONS MADE IN SEVERAL CHURCHES IN THIS TOWN."

On 6th May 1833 it was reported to the commissioners that a few days earlier Sergeant Black had been seriously assaulted outside a local inn and was unable to attend his duty. It was thought that he would be disabled for some time owing to the severity of his wounds and the commissioners appointed Charles Little as interim sergeant. Sergeant Black was later to make a full recovery as on 1st July 1833 he was re-appointed as sergeant.

On 7th July 1833 the clerk, Mr. Brown, reported that acting on the instructions of the commissioners he had advertised for six efficient men to act as police officers of the burgh. The commissioners decided to continue with Sergeant Black, Samuel Carruthers, Joseph Dunn and John Weems, but dismissed James Kirkpatrick, John Bell and George Brown appointing William Ferguson, John Copland and William Kennedy in their place.

On 6th March 1834 Sergeant Black was brought before the commissioners charged with assaulting an Italian who subsisted by examining a dancing bear on the streets. The complainer, Mr. Osborne an innkeeper of Friars Vennel reported that the Italian had been intoxicated and behaved in a disorderly manner in Friars Vennel. The police were sent for and three officers were conveying the man to the watch house when Sergeant Black joined them at the port of the Vennel and observed the prisoner struggling violently. Sergeant Black struck the man violently over the bare head with a heavy bludgeon, the man was stunned and his blood flowed copiously.

A report in the 'Journal' on the incident published on the 12th March 1830:

"LATE SERGEANT OF POLICE:-

The Commissioners of Police met on Thursday to investigate a charge against the Police Sergeant, by adjournment from Monday, when the complaint was first brought before the board. Petitions from a number of individuals of the 1st, 2nd and 4th Wards, were laid on the table ascribing in addition to the particular charge, which was the subject of investigation, charges of harsh and cruel treatment generally. Mr. Osborne was then heard in respect to the particular charge of wanton cruelty to a prisoner, an Italian, in the Vennel on Friday night, in striking him over the bare head with a heavy stick with great violence, for no cause, or at least, no cause sufficient to provoke or justify such treatment.

William Howatson, a journeyman Coachman, stated on oath that he saw a stranger (the prisoner in question) being conducted up the Vennel on Friday, about half past ten o'clock; he was struggling to get away from the officers, of whom there was one on each side of him and one behind. The prisoner had no hat or cap on. The Sergeant of Police was a few yards in advance of the party. He saw the Sergeant turn back and strike the man with great violence. The stick he employed for that purpose was a thick heavy stick. Howatson was about a dozen of yards off, but he heard the blow distinctly. The man complained, and would, he thought, have fallen to the ground, had ne not been held up. Howatson did not see any blood.

John Copeland saw the man struggling with the officers; he appeared to be tipsy, but not incapable. He did not see the blow given by the Sergeant, but he saw the prisoners head bloody.

John McNairn went out of his residence on hearing a noise, when he saw it to be occasioned by the officers conducting the Italian to the prison. He seemed to be the worse of liquor. The Sergeant was walking three or four yards behind the party. Some one of the crowd exclaimed that the prisoner was kicking, on which the Sergeant immediately turned around and struck him on the head and legs. The prisoner exclaimed against the treatment of a poor stranger. The head was all over blood. The stick was a big thick stick, and the blow a severe one; when the party got to the prison, the blood was dropping from the man's head on the stick of the policeman that led him. The night was not very dark.

Richard Taylor saw the Sergeant strike the prisoner; it was as heavy a blow as he was able to inflict. He was very close to the party at the time, and heard the blow distinctly; the stick was thick and heavy. The man cried out when struck.

William Ferguson, one of the policemen engaged on the occasion was conducting the prisoner up the Vennel when they met the Sergeant. At the time Joseph Dunn held one arm and Ferguson the other. Another officer named Wemys was pushing the prisoner from behind. When the Sergeant came up and told the prisoner that he must not strike or abuse the officers; the prisoner had been struggling to get away, but at that moment he was quiet. When the Sergeant spoke the prisoner made a kick at him; Ferguson could not say whether it took effect or not, the Sergeant was about two yards off. The instant the prisoner made to kick the Sergeant struck the prisoner severely on the head. The blood sprung from the wound. The prisoner had not struck him or Dunn previously to the Sergeant's meeting them, nor did he strike them after that. He had no hat or cap on from the beginning. The three men that had hold of him could have carried him to prison without difficulty.

*Joseph Dunn said the prisoner, while they leading him up the Vennel,
kicked him several times, but not severely; he was struggling to get away
from them. When the prisoner made to kick the Sergeant. Dunn told
the latter to stand back. The Sergeant immediately struck the prisoner
on the head. After he struck the prisoner he stated that the prisoner
had kicked his knee. There was a reddish mark on the knee then next
morning. The prisoner was tipsy and very noisy.*

*The board heard that the prisoner was brought before the court the
morning after his arrest and the court had ordered that he and his
performing bear were to be conducted beyond the bounds of the burgh.*

*The board moved to accept the Sergeant's resignation which was
accepted unanimously."*

The joy at the sergeant's departure was reported in the 'Journal' at the time:

*"This case excited considerable interest and the Council Room was
crowded during the investigation. As the Sergeant had been very
unpopular with a certain portion of the lieges, his resignation was made
the case of general rejoicing in the evening - burning of effigies etc.; and
ere the ebullition subsided breaches of the peace were committed, which
are likely to bring some of the constituents of the rabble deservedly into
trouble."*

On 12th March 1834 the following was published in the Dumfries Times:

"A Sergeant of Police Wanted and Collection of Police Assessment

*Wanted immediately, to fill up the vacancy of POLICE SERGEANT,
for this town, a stout, able bodied man. None need apply for the
office who have not first lodged, with the Clerk, proper testimonials
of the Applicant's sober and industrious habits, and civil and discreet
deportment. The salary will be at the rate of $40 sterling, per annum.*

*The Collector of Police having been instructed to collect the Police
Assessment, he will attend for receiving the same at his office, No 22
English Street, upon Thursday the 20th inst. And each succeeding
day in that week following, from 10 O'clock forenoon till four o'clock
afternoon.*

*All arrears of the Assessment at, and previous to, Whitsunday, 1833,
and the half of the Assessment from Whitsunday last, to Whitsunday
next, must be paid within the time above specified, otherwise the
defaulters will be subjected to warrants of distress.*

For the conveniency of the rate payers the other half of the latter Assessment will be received either now or at Whitsunday next.

Dumfries 10th March 1834."

On 24th March 1834 the commissioners heard the applicants for the vacant situation as sergeant of burgh police. The applicants were William Coupland, Samuel Walker, John Campbell, John Burns, Christopher Inglis and Alexander Halliday. From these men the commissioners selected William Coupland as their new sergeant.

At the meeting of 27th September that year the commissioners heard a complaint against John Dunn and Samuel Carruthers that they had acted improperly and were drunk. Both men were found guilty of the charges, found to be addicted to drunkenness and dismissed. At the same meeting the commissioners supported the magistrate's decision to dismiss John Thorburn (of whom there is no earlier mention) for being inefficient and sleeping on duty. William French, James Kilpatrick and George Armstrong were appointed in their place.

On 10th December 1834 the sergeant applied to the commissioners for handcuffs owing to the violent conduct of certain of the police offenders. The commissioners agreed and ordered three pairs for use only under the strict guidance of the Sergeant.

The above 'Police Morning Report' shows That Constables W French, J Kilpatrick, G Armstrong, C Weames, A Johnston and J Campbell were on duty on the night of 27th March 1835 and that Sergeant, William Coupland vouched for their attendance.

On 4th September 1835 the Provost stated that sundry complaints had been made to him of the very inefficiently paved state of Buccleuch Street and proposed to remedy such inconvenience that the whole of the street should be immediately 'Macadamised'.

"About 1815 John Louden McAdam recommended that roads should be lifted above the adjacent terrain to improve drainage. The surface should then be covered with large rocks and then with smaller rubble, the whole surface was then to be covered and bound with fine gravel. This was later amended to incorporate a fine layer of tar to bind the surface and dispel water to the roadside ditches."

On the 21st September 1836 the Dumfries and Galloway Courier reports:

"CHILD MURDER:

ISABELLA SHAW, or SHANE, stood accused of the unnatural crime of child murder, but as the case broke down, and as the evidence would not edify our readers, we forebear to report it. On the 17th January last, the dead body of a child was found on the Maxwelltown side of the Nith, the parentage of which was brought home to the panel. The midwife and other witnesses deponed, that the child appeared to be full grown, and was tended with care in the first instance, though the former remarked, that she did not think it would live long. Another witness who knew the prisoner hinted to her, she was afraid she was going "to play Nell Kennedy with it", when she replied, "God forbid". No water was found in the stomach or lungs, and the medical gentlemen who examined the body, and drew up a report, could not state positively that the child had not died a natural death. On this evidence the public prosecutor abandoned the case, though he conceived the proper verdict should be 'Not proven'. Mr. Carlyle addressed the jury briefly, but energetically, and looking at all the facts, weighing all the evidence, particularly that of the medical gentlemen, he conceived they could have no difficulty in returning a verdict of 'Not guilty'. After a brief charge, the jury pronounced a verdict of 'Not proven'. The prisoner was then dismissed from the bar; she was much effected, and decently dressed."

On 23rd January 1837 Sergeant Copland resigned and Robert Bell was appointed in his place. In April that year John Campbell and George Armstrong resigned their posts and John Hamilton and Gordon Heron were appointed to replace them.

After 1838 Superintendent John Bland was appointed as the Justice of the Peace Procurator Fiscal for the burgh to prosecute minor crimes outwith the reach of the sheriff court. He was also the Inspector of Weights and Measures.

In February 1839 there is the report of a robbery in Academy Street. As the result of a complaint against them by the burgh procurator fiscal, Constables John Hamilton and William French were brought before the magistrates and council to answer a charge of letting a suspect escape. Both argued that they had no reason to suspect the alleged criminal of the offence, even though he was known to be a character of bad reputation. Both were dismissed as being unfit for their present situations. Thomas Boyes and George Armstrong were later installed in their place.

On 2nd March 1839 the officers were to get new uniforms. They were to wear grey trousers, a black hat and a jacket with a red collar and a white lace trim. The sergeant was to wear the same, but in a finer material and he was to wear three chevrons on his arm to denote his rank.

In April that year Sergeant Bell was found intoxicated while on duty and was formally reprimanded. John Weems was then promoted to corporal and awarded a pay rise and two stripes to wear on his sleeve.

In October that year Gordon Heron left the service to become a keeper at the 'Crichton Institution for Lunatics' and John Campbell was appointed in his place.

On 19th February 1840 the following is reported in the Dumfries Times:

"FERCOCIOUS ATTACK

About 12 o'clock on the night of Monday last week, Dickson, a supernumerary police officer, while on duty in St Michael Street, here, was attacked and severely injured by four fellows supposed to be poachers: and had he not received assistance, it is probable he would have been murdered. The same squad also attacked, and slightly injured one of the police in English Street, on the same night."

There is reference to 'supernumerary' constables throughout the nineteenth century. There appears to have been a system in place whereby people were waiting to become constables and were sometimes employed like the present day 'special constables and supported the regular force when an officer was off sick, manpower was short or there was a special event. Supernumerary officers were also like a waiting list and they regularly became constables.

In May 1840 Charles Nelson and Thomas Boyes resigned, Nelson had obtained employment as a keeper at the Crichton Asylum. William Dickson was appointed to replace Nelson.

On 12th September 1840 Procurator Fiscal Charles McGeorge formally charged Sergeant Bell with being intoxicated while in the execution of his duty. Sergeant Bell resigned his position and William Davidson was appointed sergeant.

In December, 1840, Superintendent William Mitchell of the Dumfries County (rural) Constabulary wrote to the Dumfries Burgh Police Commissioners and requested that the burgh police officers be put under his command. He offered to take responsibility for the efficient policing of Dumfries Burgh without call for remuneration. He stated that such an amalgamation would help suppress vagrancy and prevent crime. The Police commissioners agreed to meet with Mr. Mitchell and asked him to report back to them in writing outlining his plans. There is no record of him replying in writing and the matter appears to have been dropped.

In March 1841 James Kirkpatrick and William Dickson were dismissed in a shake-up of staff. The commissioners were looking to unite the role of burgh officer and watchman and two staff had to go. Later, in July that year John Weems (or Wemys) was dismissed for being drunk and Charles Nelson appointed in his place. At this time George Armstrong was dismissed for willful falsehood and William McBurnie was appointed in his place.

On 4th May 1842 William Nelson, Master of Scavengers, Charles Higgins and John O'Neil, both scavengers, were appointed into the police to lend assistance. This was a temporary measure, although there is no record of how long this was to last. Later that month William Williamson was dismissed for an alleged assault. He was reinstated a month later when it was found that the complaint against him was grossly exaggerated and in fact the complainer was the aggressor.

This wasn't to last long as he was dismissed again on 10th October and replaced by James Allan. About this time Constable Robert Smith died in service. The commissioners discussed the plight of his widow and children. They agreed unanimously to award her £1:10:00 (£1:50p, 3 weeks wages) as Smith had been a good and efficient officer. The commissioners appointed Joseph Aitchison in his place.

During February 1843 the police officers, through their sergeant, asked for a wage rise. The commissioners discussed this at length before declining. They did, however, award all of the officers a one off payment of 10 shilling (50p) to purchase new shoes or boots. The award of boot allowance was to become a regular reimbursement in lieu of a wage rise.

On 22nd March 1843 the Dumfries and Galloway Standard was born. The newspaper was published by the Reverend Henry Duncan, Parish Minister of Ruthwell, who was also responsible for the Trustees Savings Banks. Prior to the 'Standard' there was the Dumfries and Galloway Courier which was published between 1809 and 1939. Even earlier was the Dumfries Weekly Journal which ran between 1777 and 1833, and the Dumfries Times, 1833 to 1842.

On 28th April 1843 John Campbell resigned and Maxwell Coats was appointed to replace him.

During December 1843 it is reported that Maxwell Coats and William McBurnie were suspended for some infringement, although they were later reinstated after being admonished by the commissioners.

During February 1844 each officer was awarded 15 shillings (75p) for new shoes or boots.

On 28th June 1844 Provost Crichton reported that Maxwell Coats had resigned. William Dickson was appointed in his place.

Superintendent John Jones

Chapter three
SUPERINTENDENT JOHN JONES

During the meeting of commissioners of 26th July 1844 it was revealed that on 15th May 1844 Provost Crichton had approached Superintendent John Jones of the Dumfries County Police asking for advice as to the running of a proper police force in the burgh. Mr. Jones who had commenced his police career with the Metropolitan Police, before being appointed Superintendent of Dumfries County Police in 1843 replied with a long list of issues that were to become the rules and regulation of the burgh police.

John Jones was born at Lambeth, London in 1814. He was superintendent (and later chief constable) of the Dumfries County Police from 1843 to 1891. He died at Dumfries in 1897

When appointed as superintendent of the county police, John Jones was a single man, 29 years of age and spent a large part of his youth in Wales. He was a sergeant in the Metropolitan Police having joined the newly re-organised metropolitan police service when he was sixteen. The Metropolitan Police (Sir Robert Peel's 'Peelers') were formed as a result of the Metropolitan Police Act 1829.

Sir Richard Maine, one of the two joint Commissioners of Police of the Metropolis, had personally recommended Sergeant Jones for the post in reply to a letter from the Duke of Buccleuch who had written to the Commissioners of Police, on behalf of the Dumfries County Police Board, asking for a sound candidate for the post.

John Jones travelled to Dumfries, rented accommodation in English Street, Dumfries, a short walk from his office in what is now Militia House, English Street part of the Dumfries and Galloway Council Buildings and attended his first county Police Board meeting of 22nd November 1843.

On August 29th 1844 the council met and a discussion relative to the merits of Mr. Jones was discussed:

> *"The suggestions for improving the police force of the burgh were then brought before the meeting by the Provost, who moved the appointment of a committee to revise them prior to them being adopted. Mr. Dunbar objected to the recommendation that Mr. Jones of the county police should have the 'superintendence of the burgh force, to see the alterations carried into effect'; and was supported by Mr. Hammond. Provost Crichton alleged that this was not the case, as had been erroneously stated in one of the newspapers, and the clause in question was then read by the Clerk. It was as follows: "That Mr. Jones. Sergeant to the Dumfries Constabulary Force be requested to take the superintending charge of seeing the above suggestions carried*

into effect, and report from time to time". The Provost added that it was not intended to place Mr. Jones above the burgh Sergeant, but that the two should act in concert, under the direction and advise from the magistrates. Baillie Newall proposed that the matter should be submitted to an open committee with a small quorum. Mr. Dunbar wished to have the opinion of Sergeant Dawson, who averred that he did not want any assistance in the discharge of his duty: that the new regulations were just those that had been in force in London for a considerable number of years; but that while they suited London, they would not do for Dumfries.; and was proceeding to read from a paper a series of objections against them when he was told that these had better be laid before the committee which would be appointed. Mr. Scott though that Mr. Jones was the very person to be over both Sergeant and men. The Provost repeated that it was not wished to take the power out of the Sergeant's hands, but to assist him, and instanced an occasion upon which, during the illness of Sergeant Dawson, and the misconduct of the substitute, Mr. Jones had rendered effective aid. Mr. Jones would also be better able to do his duty in the county, by having the cooperation of the town police. After a lengthy and rather warm discussion, Dean Irving proposed that the suggestions should be now adopted; but ultimately the motion of Baillie Newall, to refer these to a committee of the whole commissioners was agreed to, the committee to meet on Monday at 7 o'clock, 3 being a quorum."

On 3rd September 1844 Provost Fraser, Bailies Nicholson and Thomson, together with commissioners McGeorge, Newall, Irving, Sinclair, Johnstone, Hamilton, McGowan and Smith met within the council chambers and agreed to the following rules and regulations as suggested by Mr. Jones:

"Suggestions for Improvements in the Town Police of Dumfries:

1) Of the Force in general.

It is recommended that one additional man be added to the force, making a total of six men including the Sergeant.

DAY DUTIES

The duty to be performed by these men to be as follows: Two men to be on duty from 6 morning till 9 at night - thus one man to go at six and remain till 9 in the morning, at which hours to be relieved for breakfast and to return at ten to attend the court and any other duties that may be required of him to go on duty again at three afternoon and relieve that man that was on at nine and remain on duty till 9 PM. The man who went off at three to return at five or six (according to the season of the year) and remain also till 9 PM when the streets are generally throngest, these men to be relieved at 9 PM by the men for

NIGHT DUTY

The three men for the night duty to muster at quarters to 9PM and after being inspected by the Sergeant despatched to their respective districts, which should be named by the sergeant previous to their leaving the office and these to patrol till the morning and accept on market days when the whole force should be available if found necessary. It is impossible that under the present regulations men can perform their duty with efficiency or with spirit. The hours they are asked to be on duty being too many which causes them to be lax in the performance of it and to patrol their districts without that care and inspection absolutely necessary in a night Watchman. Altho by the above plan the night duty men would be reduced in number yet it would be found that the services of the police would be far more efficient than at present.

CALLING THE HOURS

This practice ought to be dropped as it is frought with dangers to the property as opposed to the judicious performance of police duties. It may be said that it gives a feeling of security to the inhabitants and proves that the Watchmen is at least not asleep and shews where he is, but it plainly shews where he is not and if it operates as a warning to depredators from one part of the district, it must equally be an invitation to other parts of it.

RATTLES AND LANTERNS

Similar to those used by the London Police force have lately been introduced and it is hoped that they will prove serviceable.

MODE OF PATROLLING THE DISTRICT

The district ought to be patrolled in a regular progressive manner and within a specified time - previous to the Constables going on duty (if at night) the Sergeant should give him instructions whether to work his district right or left - in other words whether to keep his right or left shoulder to the wall. The object of this is to render their movements uncertain to parties watching them. Thus perhaps the Sergeant will order the Constable to work his district to the right till 12 o' clock and to the left till 2 and so on during the night, thereby effecting a complete change in the motions of the Constable. The Sergeant knowing the way the men are working and can at all times find them by coming in an opposite direction. The mode is of considerable utility and by it many a Burglar has been detected in the very middle of his depredations.

BOOKS

The Sergeant ought not to have it in his power to liberate a prisoner after the charge has been entered, unless on security found that he will appear and answer to the charge when called on to do so.

2nd. A Book called an 'Occurrence Book' in which should be entered all daily occurrences: (An example is shown with four columns with the name of the accused, the date of the offence the complaint and how disposed of.)

These Books would be found to be of use and could easily be kept by the Sergeant.

When information of a serious theft is received at the Town Police Office no time should be lost in giving intimation of it at the County Police Office so that the assistance and co-operation of the officers of that force resident in Dumfries maybe secured.

2) SERGEANT'S DUTY

The Sergeant to obey and give strict attention to any orders issued by the Commissioners of Police to have full command over the men composing the force for whose good conduct he will be held responsible to the commissioners - to make himself acquainted with the character of each officer, being careful to note every case of disobedience, neglect, misconduct and to enter same in the occurrence book at all times setting an example of alacrity and skill in the discharge of duties - to be at the office on all occasions of the men going on and coming off duty, observing that they are sober and properly dressed and have all of their appointments (handcuffs, baton, lantern etc) with them - to hold no idle or familiar conversation with his men. Familiarity on the part of a Sergeant soon generates a corresponding want of respect on that of the Constable who feeling that his delinquencies are overlooked in most cases not even thought of by his superior at length loses all idea of deference and altogether neglects or at least but imperfectly performs the duties entrusted to his charge.

3) OFFICERS ON DUTY

Each Constable must devote his whole time and abilities to the service of the establishment and give strict obedience to the Orders of the Sergeant, at all times appear neat and clean in his person and correctly dressed in the establishment uniform. His demeanour must be always respectful and when going on duty must be at the office at the prescribed time and if for night duty to have all his appointments with him. He ought to make himself acquainted with every street, wynde, close etc. in his district and acquire such a knowledge of the inhabitants as will enable him to recognise them in case they should require his assistance. He must visit every part of his beat in the allocated time and regularly so that any person requiring his assistance may easily find him. So if at any time he requires immediate assistance and cannot in any other way obtain it, he must spring his rattle but he is not on any account to leave the spot where his assistance is required, and when he has any occasion to take any person into custody he must endeavour to see the adjoining Constable that he may watch his district till he returns which he is to do as soon as possible. When on duty he must not enter public houses or dram shops accept when it is legally necessary in the course of his duty. He must be particularly cautious not to interfere unnecessarily never suffering himself to be moved to passion in the slightest degree by abusive language used towards him and at all times bearing in mind that one of the most important and indisputable qualifications of a police officer is a perfect command of temper.

4)

It is suggested that Mr. Jones, Superintendent to the Dumfries County Force be requested to take a Superintending charge of seeing the above suggestions carried into effect and to report from time to time.

5) POLICE ROOMS AND LOCKUP

These places are in a filthy state and should undergo a thorough cleaning. The office would be improved by being divided by a partition. One apartment for the Sergeant and the other for the officers. The Sergeant would thus keep more aloof from the officers and take down charges and declarations through and opening in the partition without coming as at present into actual contact with the parties. The beds now used should be discontinued and guard beds made solely of wood installed. Neither straw nor blankets should be used as they tend to create vermin and rugs should be got instead which should be kept by the Sergeant and given out to prisoners only when found necessary. No one should be allowed to enter or loiter in any of the apartments accept such as are on business and these should not be allowed to remain longer than necessary. Neither should any person be admitted to see a person unless when it is indispensable. Under no circumstances should smoking or tipling be allowed either in the offices or other rooms.

Dumfries 2 September 1844

What is written upon the eleven preceding pages is the rules and regulations adopted by the commissioners of Police for the Guidance of their officers at their meeting held in the Council Chambers this day and the same is ordered to be entered in the Minute Book of the

commissioners and the Sergeant and Officers are hereby instructed to act
up to these regulations from this date and until further notice.

Signed Thomas Crichton (Provost of Dumfries)"

On 14th September 1844 Provost Crichton called a special meeting of the commissioners for the purpose of choosing two police officers. Joseph Aitchison was, at this time, suspended and was summarily dismissed.

There were a large number of candidates and after a full round of discussions the commissioners selected Benjamin Dickson and David Armstrong.

On 4th October that year Superintendent Jones wrote to the commissioners:

"To the commissioners of Police for Dumfries

Gentlemen

I beg leave to inform you that in accordance with your request at your meeting of September last I have began to see the suggestions then adopted by you for the improvement of the police carried into effect.

It is not my intention at present to lay before you a report of the progress made in the improvements - my sole object being bring unto your notice the conduct of Sergeant Dawson.

Since I became engaged in seeing the improvements proceeded with instead of accessing the full and friendly co-operation of the sergeant so necessary in the matter. I have not only met with opposition but received treatment in many instances of a most unbecoming and insulting nature from him. The following are a few instances of the conduct complained of:-

1st A few days after my interference I was in the Police House attending with the Sergeant to take forward the change; and I was surprised to find that a charge of malicious mischief which was made at the station house on the previous night was not brought forward; and asked the Sergeant, why this had not been done.   He answered that it was not a charge to bring before a police court; and upon my putting further questions to him relative to the same case he in the most incautious manner turned away and refused to answer my questions. This was observed by one or two members of the court. The case referred to was on the following day brought by the Sergeant before the sitting Magistrate, who disposed of it and fined the offender in the sum of 5 shillings.

2nd   On the morning of Thursday the 2nd September (the day after the Fair and the Town being very busy) the Sergeant and I consulted together at the Station House and agreed the disposal of the men during the day. And among other things it was arranged that Moffat a supernumerary should remain and do duty at the station house. This being one of the new arrangements and acted upon since my interference. Immediately on my leaving the Sergeant ordered Moffat from the station house, locked the door and carried the key with him. I saw this and asked the Sergeant the cause of it.   When he answered in a violent and incautious manner that he would place and take off the men and do as he thought proper and he immediately turned and walked away.

3rd   On the evening of the dance day (Thursday 2nd September) I was in the station house about 7 o'clock along with Baillie Newall when the Sergeant entered and in a violent and insolent manner asked (addressing me, who alone he observed at the time) "What's the matter here what's all this about" and immediately thereafter he observed the presence of Councillor Newall and begged his pardon. He was evidently the worse for drink.

4th   On Sunday last I was in the station house and was giving directions to the officers that they were not to idle away their time together, when the Sergeant contradicted me by saying that it was a foolish order. I told him it was not my order but that of the Commissioners; on which he said he wanted nothing to say to me, and wished to know when I was going to leave the station house by asking "Anyone going out of here".

These are a few instances of the Sergeant's conduct but I may in addition state, that several complaints have been made to me of the Sergeant being drunk; and I have been informed that on the Fair night he appeared in Mr. Sinclair's shop much the worse for liquor and this was noticed by Mr. Sinclair and Mr. Scott.

I feel it a disagreeable duty thus to report to you, but I find that it will be impossible to carry out your orders, so long as such conduct on the part of the Sergeant is allowed to continue.

I Have the Honour to be
Gentlemen
Your Obedient, Humble Servant

Signed 'John Jones'"

As a result of this letter Sergeant Dawson was called before the commissioners and instructed that in future he was to take his orders from Mr. Jones.

On 18th October 1844 Provost Crichton reported that he had suspended Sergeant Dawson for being absent from duty. By a unanimous vote of the commissioners he was reprimanded and reinstated.

The Burgh Commissioners of Police met on 29th November 1844 and elected a police officer as James Allan resigned. Petitions from the candidates were read and after considerable discussion the commission chose Francis Davidson from Duncow. The commissioners then heard the first report from Mr. Jones of the County Police. The report embraced the state of the burgh police when he undertook the superintendence.

He suggested that the commissioners give him the power to fine the officers not more than £2 for minor offences. He also recommended that the day officers be given a great coat and that no constables should be able to nominate a substitute in their place. He also suggested that homeless persons should not be allowed to pass the night in the station house. All of these suggestions were accepted by the commissioners.

He reported that at first the force, which consisted of a sergeant and five men lacked co-operation and discipline. However, these issued had been resolved and the men were much more zealous in their duties.

On 27th December 1844 Francis Davidson was dismissed at the request of Superintendent Jones for being drunk on duty. He was replaced by Constable Robert Wilson.

In February 1845 David Armstrong was dismissed for being drunk on duty and being found in the company of a common prostitute.

In March that year Charles Fraser, James Waterson and William Moffat were appointed as constables. They were also subject of a new rule. That any officer resigning should give the commissioners one month's notice and return their equipment. There is also reference to as Sergeant Wilson, who may have been a supernumerary.

On 29th August 1845 Sergeant Dawson was dismissed for misconduct and he was replaced as sergeant by James Waterson. Robert Findlay of Stranraer had been offered the post but declined asking for a higher wage. The commissioners didn't take long to select another candidate and in fact reduced the Sergeant's weekly wage by one shilling (5p).

In October that year William Moffat was dismissed and was replaced by Maxwell Coats while on 30th January 1846 Charles Fraser resigned and was replaced by James Allan.

On 26th January, 1846 it is reported that Maxwell Coats was off sick with typhus fever. The commissioners agreed to continue paying his wages only if he produced a medical certificate.

On 29th May 1846 there was a motion to dismiss Superintendent Jones. The motion was carried in full and a committee was set up to look at the policing of the town, meanwhile Superintendent Jones was left in charge of the burgh constables. At this time John Smith was dismissed for persistent drunkenness and John Handsby was employed in his place.

On 26th March 1847 Maxwell Coats and James Allan both resigned and James Stewart appointed.

The General Police (Scotland) Act, 1847 (10 & 11 Vict. c.39) was introduced and reduced the majority of householders required to adopt the police system from three quarters to two thirds. It also allowed the parliamentary burghs to adopt the burgh police act, and to levy for moneys to carry out municipal government.

In February 1848 Constables McBurnie and Stewart were both suspended for neglect of duty in letting a prisoner escape. Both were reinstated after a hearing before the commissioners. Stewart wasn't to last long as he was dismissed in March that year for being drunk on duty. Alexander McConnell was appointed in his place. McConnell obviously didn't like the job as he resigned a month later and was replaced by William Dickson.

On 16th February 1848 the Dumfries and Galloway Standard reported:

"THE SAUT BOX – ALLEGED CASE OF ILL TREATMENT

There is a letter in the 'Courier' of yesterday, signed 'Beta', which we are authorized to state gives the wrong version of a recent police case. 'Beta's' account is as follows:

"On Saturday 1st January, last, a man, residing in Queensberry Street, here, being in a state of intoxication, was apprehended on suspicion of having committed a breach of the peace, and lodged in the 'saut box, where he remained until the Monday following, when he was taken before the police court: but the plaintiff failing to appear, he was liberated. Thus, he was incarcerated in a dungeon for upwards of 36 hours without proper food (if any), the floor and walls cold and clammy, the air fetid, and into which the light of heaven is never allowed to shine – all this during very cold weather. He had lain on the floor or some other equally ungenial spot. These are the facts; and the following statements which I have to make are also true. Whether or not the first were the cause of the last, it is not for me to say positively; but it can hardly be doubted that a strong connection exists between them. He was seized by inflammation on the following Wednesday; and being of rather a lust nature, dropsy succeeded. He lingered out till Friday morning last, when death put a period to his existence: a young family has been left to deplore his loss. Who, in all likelyhood, will be thrown upon the parochial funds for the means of subsistence"

The true history of the affair is supplied to us in the following terms:

"On the Saturday specified, a complaint was made at the police office of a serious assault committed by one McIvor, a pensioner, on a labored called Maxwell; and in consequence, Mr. Jones dispatched three officers, Nelson, Coutts and Tweedie, to inquire into the case, and, if need be, apprehend the offender, a stout, able bodied man. They found Maxwell in such a state that he could not be removed: he was much bruised and was literally dripping with blood from the results of the assault he had suffered. On enquiry being made at his daughter regarding the affray, she stated that her father had gone into McIvor's house, and that they had there quarreled; she heard the former crying out loudly, but McIvor had bolted the door and no one could get entrance till some time afterwards. The cause of the quarrel she was unable to state. The officers then took McIvor, who was tipsy, into custody, brought him to the police office, where he sergeant examined him, and took down the case. When the prisoner was asked why he had abused the man, he said he had affronted him and if anyone had come in, he would have treated him the same way. The evidence was strong against him, there were no exculpatory statements made by any party, and there was no alternative left but to keep him in the office till Monday morning for trial. He was put into one of the cells of the 'saut box', but instead of remaining there 36 hours, as stated above, he was confined there only one hour, and during that period had the use of blankets sent from his home. At the end of an hour he was brought upstairs to what is called the side room, a place which, if not an enviable residence, is at least as comfortable as any of the cells at the Dumfries prison. Here he was kept until Monday morning, having meanwhile been supplied with proper food and at 10 o'clock was brought up before Baillie Hammond, who found the evidence of a contradictory nature. The chief witness (Maxwell) who suffered the assault, could not attend, he was still too ill and a certificate from Dr. Scott to this effect having been produced; while the prisoner's father in law gave evidence which tended to show that Maxwell and not McIvor had commenced the quarrel. The evidence being of such a nature, the presiding Magistrate dismissed the case, and the prisoner was set at large. He was seen out two or three days afterwards, as healthy in appearance as ever, but often in a dissipated state, he having drawn his pension about the time. After that he was seized with 'erysipelas, of which it is believed he died, and was buried on Sabbath week, his wife having died a few days before of a similar disease. This is a melancholy tale, and, if our informants are to be relied upon, the true one, though differing in many essential points from the account given by 'Beta'. "

"Granting the statements given to us to be correct which we believe that are, there appears to be no good ground for supposing that there was any connection between the poor man's confinement and his death, though

we think, to remove all suspicion, and as the charge implied is such a serious one, the subject should be closely and searchingly investigated by the legal authorities."

In October 1848 the Committee selected to look into the policing of the town reported back to the commissioners. They recommended that the commissioners should appoint a superintendent of town police who would be exclusively responsible for the policing of the town. Superintendent Jones continued to monitor the burgh force with daily visits to the station house and instructions in the general order book.

The following appears in the general order book on 1st April 1849:

Report – 1st April 1849

PC Alexander McConnell has made application to the Superintendent to resign his situation as Police Officer in the Burgh of Dumfries. It is desired by the Superintendent that his intention as to resigning should be entered in the Occurrence Book and presented to the Magistrates as the said PC Alexander McConnell is desirous of leaving his situation as Police Office on Wednesday the 4th current. As a situation has been offered to him at the present time, which might not occur for a length of time again.

On 6th April 1849 PC McConnell was granted his wish to resign and was replaced by supernumerary Constable William Dickson.

On 7th May 1849 the burgh police consisted of:

"Sergeant Waterston and Constable Allan on day duty
Acting Sergeant Wilson, Constable Handsby, Constable McBurnie and Constable Dickson on night duty."

Superintendent Jones visited the station house virtually every day and regularly twice a day. On each visit he would make an entry on the general order book:

"I certify that I visited this station at (time) and found all correct (or otherwise dependent on what he found)."

On 6th July 1849 Constable John Hansby was the subject of a complaint:

"Mr. Hugh McClure, engineer, has given in a complaint about PC John Hansby with being the worse of drink and abusive language, injuring his body, clothes and person, on the High Street when on duty between the hours of 2 and 3 O'clock on the morning of 5th July 1849."

There is no record of the case being investigated by the superintendent or being report to the magistrates.

On 13th September 1849 Superintendent Jones reported the Sergeant for being absent from duty:

"On visiting the station at different times between the hours of 1/20 and 31/2 pm the sergeant on duty was not to be found he having gone to his dinner. On making enquiries it was found that he had removed from the council chambers and only slept there at night. The Sgt. explained that his daughter was ill and that he was at a house in English Street where she resided. John Jones Supt."

On 1st August 1849 Sergeant Waterston was again in trouble:

Sergeant Waterston absent from station from 12 0'clock until 20 minutes to 3 o'clock afternoon on 30th July 1849 and returned at that time much the worse of liquor. Witnesses, R Wilson and Constable Burnie."

Later that night Superintendent Jones visited the station:

"This station was visited by me at 9 pm and all was correct except as above stated and having made further enquiries find that the Sergeant "Waterston" is at times much confused and unfit for duty."

On 2nd August 1849 Superintendent Jones reported:

"The Supt. having consulted the Magistrates gave intimation that Sergeant Waterston was suspended till further notice or until the Police Commissioners met. He was warned accordingly. John Jones."

Later that day the matter was finally resolved:

"On a complaint by the Supt to the Magistrates this day against PS James Waterston for being frequently drunk and neglect of duty, the Sergeant resigned his station, and the Supt. was directed to get a Sgt. In his place till the next meeting of the Commissioners."

On 28th August 1849 the Superintendent received a letter of complaint from William Grierson:

"Dear Sir
I am afraid you begin to think of me as troublesome to you in your official capacity; but being fully aware that you have no wish to shrink from doing your duty, I would earnestly recommend you to exercise your authority, in putting down that intolerable and disgusting practice

which a set of the most abandoned and disorderly characters of both sexes have of assembling regularly every Saturday evening at the head of Swans Vennel, where they carry on their orgies during the whole of the night and even to a late hour on the Sunday morning, to the annoyance and disturbance of the whole neighbourhood. I understand that those persons to whom license is permitted to sell drink are by an order of the Magistrates. Strictly enjoined to close their doors at ten o'clock. If this is really the case surely that most respectable bench will never consent to stand by, with their eyes open, and permit their authority to be treated with contempt and open defiance. Yet certain it is that those disorderly characters of which I complain do obtain drink at all hours from the house in the immediate neighbourhood.

I appears to me therefore, that the Magistrates would only be consistently supporting their dignity if they were at once to deprive that and every such house of their license and our hope is that you will vigourously employ your authority in ridding the public of this growing evil. I am with all due respect, Dear Sir
Yours Most Truly
Wm. Grierson."

On 7th October 1849 an entry appears in the general order book as William Waterston the former sergeant returns:

"James Waterston was ordered to take charge of the Burgh Police of Dumfries until further orders by order of the Provost on the 7th October 1848. J. Waterstone."

On 3rd October 1849 the Commissioners of Police met:

"COMMISSIONERS OF POLICE

An ordinary monthly meeting of this body was held on Friday last, Provost Kennedy in the chair. ….
The subject of appointing a new Serjeant to the Burgh police force was then introduced, and several applications for the vacant office were laid upon the table. Mr. McNab of Annan, was spoken of by Dean Mundell and Baillie Harkness as a very desirable officer to obtain for serjeant. Baillie Nicholson was of the opinion that improvements in the management of the force were required, and that it would be well if the whole system were brought under consideration with a view to having it remodelled. Possibly they might be able to manage without Mr. Jones; and by giving a serjeant a better salary, and imposing upon him the whole charge, and advantage might be obtained. Baillie Harkness took a similar view of the subject. He urged the necessity for some change being adopted, and thought the one referred to would be attended with the best results. The Superintendent of the county police had a great

deal to do in watching over such a great breadth of country, and it was essentially requisite that an officer should be obtained to devote his undivided attention to the affairs of the burgh. On the motion of Mr. Dunbar, the subject was remitted to the consideration of the magistrates; and the meeting adjourned.

On 10th October 1849 the Commissioners of Police met:

"COMMISSIONERS OF POLICE

The report of the Magistrates regarding the superintendence of the Police force was read. It was in the following terms:-

Report of the Provost, Magistrates, Dean of Guild, and Treasurer, upon a Remit by the Commissioners of Police of Dumfries, as to the Burgh Police Force, and testimonials for an Officer to occupy the vacant office of Serjeant.

Your committee have given the whole subject their best consideration, and now report the result of their investigations.

The Committee, while satisfied of the great importance of a good understanding and cooperation between the officers of the County Police and those of the Burgh, and while expressing, as they entertain, thanks for the time and trouble spent by Mr. Jones, Superintendent of the County Police, in affording a superintendence over the Burgh Police, according to the time and opportunities which his extensive and arduous duties in the County could afford, are nevertheless of opinion that the Burgh Police Force require reinvigoration, and more especially the appointment of a well qualified Superintendent, whose time and exertions shall be exclusively applied within Burgh, not only in the protection of life and property, and the repressing of crime, but in aid of the Magistrates, Conveners of Committees, and other members of the Town Council, and Board of Police Commissioners in reference to the inspection and prosecution of nuisances , the watching, cleansing, and paving of the streets, and preservation of the town's property.

That is the opinion of your committee, that in selecting a new Sergeant or Superintendent of Police, regard should be paid to the importance of such and officer taking the general superintendence of these matters; the salary to be paid, therefore, being to be increased to 20 shillings (£1) per week, part to be paid by the Town Council such being an increase upon the allowance of 25 shillings per week now paid by the Commissioners of Police.

Having regard to these principles, your Committee further report that they have examined the testimonials laid before them in favour of various candidates; and referring to the personal appearance made, and explanations given, by William McNab, Burgh and Criminal Officer in Annan, in connection with string recommendations from C. Stewart Esq, Hillside, The Provost and Magistrates of Annan, Sheriff Trotter, Mr. Young, Procurator Fiscal of Dumfries, and others, the Committee recommend the Commissioners of Police to engage William McNab as Superintendent of the Burgh Police, on the conditions before explained; and in doing so, they beg to express their earnest desire that the best of feeling and cooperation may be maintained among the officers of the County and Burgh to prosecute general efficiency, so as to tend to the repression of crime, to accomplish which the authorities of the Burgh will exert their best endeavours.

Mr. Dunbar, seconded by Mr. Smith, moved the adoption and approval of the report. Mr. Dinwiddie thought the Committee had exceeded their powers in making any new arrangements about the inspection of nuisances. No one person was competent to superintend the police, and do this extra duty with efficiency besides. Mr. Balieff was dissatisfied with the report: on another account. He was convinced that the police would suffer wanting the services of Mr. Jones. At the time when that gentleman took the superintendence of the police, they were in a disgraceful condition of inefficiency; and he (Mr. Balieff) thought it was scarcely courteous to dismiss a man from the force so summarily, who had been the means of bringing it to its present efficiency. He had never understood that the Committee had to do anything more than appoint a serjeant, leaving the superintendence to stand as formerly. Baillie Harkness stated that, though the minute appointing the Committee (which was read at Mr. Balieffs request) might be technically deficient inasmuch as it did not directly specify the superintendence of the police as the subject of their inquiry, yet all who were present at the time it was appointed were aware that the Committee were to consider this in connection with the filling up of the vacant office of Serjeant. Mr. Harkness went on to show that the arrangement recommended by the Committee was considered by them to be necessary for the benefit of the town, and that they had come to this conclusion not out of disrespect for Mr. Jones, to whom they had awarded the highest praise, but because he had other arduous and engrossing duties to attend to. After some more discussion on the subject, Mr. Balieff moved, and Mr. Fraser seconded, an amendment dissaproving of the report: and on a vote being taken, no votes were recorded for the amendment – eleven Commissioners viting for the motion, and the others present, including Mr. Balieff, abstaining from voting. In reply to a question from Mr. Dinwiddie, it was stated that the point regarding the appointment of an inspector would be regulated at a future meeting."

On 24th October the Commissioners of Police met yet again:

"COMMISSIONERS OF POLICE

The usual monthly meeting of this body was held on the 19th current, instead of Friday next, that day being the Saturday. Provost Kennedy in the chair.

The Clerk intimated that Mr. McNab had accepted office as Superintendent of Police. He was then sworn in: and in reply to Baillie Harkness, he stated the regular force consisted of six men, including himself; and that Mr Waterston had, at the suggestion of the Provost, been for the time appointed Sergeant as before.

A communication was read from Mr. Jones acknowledging the receipt of the remit on the Committee and expressed his thanks to the Committee for their praise of his past service, but regretted the manner in which their agreement with him had been terminated. Mr. Scott regretted very much that he had been absent from the preceding meeting where they had resolved on dismissing Mr. Jones in such a summary way. He thought it would have been much more businesslike, and certainly far more courteous, if the magistrates had just sent for Mr. Jones, and conferred with him upon the subject. This would have been a course of conduct such as gentlemen ought to pursue to each other. He had not seen the report, but from all he could learn, Mr. Jones had not been well used. His dismissal was a triumph to those who did not approve of him, particularly to the rabble. He, Mr. Scott, regretted very much that they had lost the services of Mr. Jones, which had been very valuable to the burgh. Baillie Harkness said he had no desire to enter into a fresh discussion on a matter which had been calmly entertained and decided, and he certainly thought it was a pity that Mr. Scott had not been present before, or at all events had not read the report of the Magistrates, which contained ample vindication of their decision. It would have been well if Mr. Scott, instead of drawing his conclusion from Mr. Jones' letter, had seen the report, which would have altered his views considerably and hindered him from casting undeserved reflections on the bench. Mr. Scott repeated his previous statement, adding that the Committee, as they would not wish their own feelings to be hurt, should have paid more deference to those of others. Mr. Dunbar expressed his surprise at Mr. Scott's observations and assured him that no one had wished to get quit of Mr. Jones, as he seemed to think, their parting with him having been brought about by the statements of Mr. McNab that he could not think of taking the charge of the force unless he had full control over it. It had also been found by experience that the past practice had not worked well. Mr. Dawson had given satisfaction so long as he had full authority, but as soon as Mr. Jones was set over him his usefulness declined, and they were forces to part with him. Mr. Waterston's efficiency had also been affected by this system, for when the Sergeants were placed under a Superintendent they were rendered dependent, and their hands trammelled. When a change was made, it was solely for the purpose of rendering the force more efficient, and out of no ill feeling whatever towards Mr. Jones. The arrangement was made in a calm, deliberate and equitable way. The Provost said that what was done was the act of the Commissioners at large, who had received the report of the Magistrates sitting in committee and had approved of it. Mr. Scott had all along been against the practice of naming the Magistrates on committees, and had he been present, he would certainly have opposed it in this instance. In regard to the matter more immediately under consideration, he had to say that his views had not changed. He had talked over it to individual Commissioners, and they had admitted that the proceeding he had condemned was deficient in courtesy."

Chapter Four
SUPERINTENDENT WILLIAM MCNABB

On 19th October 1849 William McNabb aged 38 years was appointed as the first dedicated superintendent of police of Dumfries. McNabb was married to Mary McNabb and they had seven children. Mary-Ann and William were born in Ireland. Henry and Adam were born at Lockerbie, Catherine and Letticia were born at Annan and Richard who was born at Dumfries.

McNabb was born 1810 in Dublin and had come to the area from the Metropolitan Police Dublin in 1843 when he was appointed as the first rural Inspector of police at Thornhill in the then newly formed Dumfries County Police. He had also been inspector at Lockerbie. At the time of his appointment as superintendent of police, Mr. McNabb was employed as a Burgh and Criminal Officer at Annan. On 26th December 1849 the general order book contains the following entry by Superintendent McNabb:

> *"Sergeant James Waterston reported for being absent from the council chambers when instructed as a witness of W. Bailieff against John Hansby(or Handby) on the evening of Wednesday the 26th at 6 o'clock and when he appeared after being repeatedly sent for he was under the influence of drink and unfit to be examined as a witness in the case. Further for being absent from duty at 9 pm when he should have been at the station house ready for duty and when he came afterwards he was under the influence of drink and unfit for duty. Consequently he was suspended by order of Baillie Dickie he being duty magistrate."*

On the 28th December James Waterston was dealt with by the magistrates for his conduct:

> *"At a meeting of the Commissioners of Police the above report was read and Sergt. Waterston being called to answer to the complaint plead guilty and by order of the Board by a majority was ordered to be dismissed."*

In January 1850 Robert Kerr, William Richardson and Francis O'Neil were appointed as constables. John Dickson resigned while James Kirkpatrick and John Muir appointed. Francis O'Neil was unmarried, 21 years of age and stayed in Friars Vennel with his sister.

The Police of Towns (Scotland) Act, 1850 (13 & 14 Vict. c.33) also known as "Lock's Act" repealed much of the earlier legislation. It also made it easier for police burghs to be created. Any "populous place" was now allowed to adopt a police system and become a burgh. A populous place was defined as any town, village, place or locality not already a burgh and with a population of 1,200 inhabitants or upwards. At the same time, a poll in favour of adopting the act now needed only a simple majority.

On February 20th 1850 the superintendent brought in Sergeant John Carroll and Constables Adam Bell and Thomas Wilson and had them sworn in as constables. It can only be assumed that these men were supernumerary officers.

May 5th 1850 Superintendent McNabb reports:

"Constable number 3, Robert Kerr, was charged by James Wilson, broker of Queensberry Street, Dumfries, with entering his house between 11 and 12 o'clock on the night of Friday the 3rd May without any proper reason or any cause for a police officer to do so and thereby annoying him and at the time being under the influence of drink . This case was tried before Baillie Dickie and proven. Kerr was fined 5 shillings or to be suspended for one week."

In June 1850 Sergeant Carroll resigned and was replaced by Francis O'Neil and Constable John Slimmin was appointed as sergeant. The 1851 Census identifies a Police Sergeant John Slimmin a 30 year old bachelor, living with his mother in Academy Street, Dumfries. John Slimmin's death is reported in the Standard on 1st January 1853.

In July Adam Bell resigned and was replaced by Thomas Templeton was appointed in his place.

On July 18th Superintendent McNabb reports:

"Police Constable William Richardson was reported by Mr. John Smythe, writer, for being drunk on duty. He was brought in off his beat and the superintendent found that he was drunk and placed another man on duty in his place. He was brought before Baillie Scott and admitted his offence and was fined 2 shillings and sixpence and reprimanded."

On July 31st John Dickson applied for a situation in the burgh police and produced his discharge from Lancashire Constabulary, his character being good he was admitted. He resigned in December 1852. As a result the superintendent reported as follows:

"The superintendent reports the resignation of John Dickson and the vacancy open by an order of the town council at their last meeting to add another constable to the force which left two vacancies and he

*brought four candidates forward viz. James Kirkpatrick, John Muir,
Alexander Edgar and James Kennedy of whom the commissioners
selected Kirkpatrick and Muir and swore them in as supernumerary
constables which made the whole force complete."*

On 4th December 1850 the commissioners of police met:

"COMMISSIONER OF POLICE

*An ordinary meeting of the Police Board was held on Friday. Present:
Provost Nicholson, in the chair, Baillies Leighton and Scott, and Messrs.
W Dickie, Currie, Dinwiddie, Clark, Black, Crombie, Gibson, Harkness,
Blaind, Murray, McGowan and Balieff.*

*Superintendent McNabb's report was then read. It stated that, in
accordance with permissions granted to him he had remodeled the police
force, and had found the change to operate beneficially. The conduct
of the new constables had been good. Crime had decreased in the
town, and comparatively few cases had been handed over to the county
fiscal. In order to place the force on a proper footing, however, it would
be requisite hat its strength should be increased by the addition of one
man, as the duties performed by the present number were too arduous
and incompatible with the men's health, not to say comfort. The cost
at present was £3 and 8 shillings per week, while that of the 'scavenging
department cost £1 and 3 shillings per week more. The Superintendent
suggested that the cleansing force should also be remodelled and placed
under the superintendent of the police, and by this means he considered
that a man's wages might be saved in the scavenging and made to
defray the expense of one constable and again, by this plan, if approved
of, the town would be better watched and cleaned at no additional cost.*

*Mr. Bland and Mr. Dinwiddie spoke approvingly of the suggestion. Mr.
Black was in favour of having an extra policeman, but would leave
the other parts of the report for further consideration. Baillie Scott
conceived the plan proposed a most excellent one. In most other towns
the cleansing and watching formed one concern, and he did not doubt
but that the former would be done far more promptly and efficiently if
placed under the superintendence of the police. The report was carried
unanimously."*

On January 1st. 1851 Sergeant Slimmin reported:

*"Between the hours of 12 o'clock and 1 o'clock on the night of
Wednesday the 1st January or morning of Thursday 2nd January,
Constable James Kirkpatrick absented himself from his beat and
when found by the sergeant he was unable to discharge his duty being
drunk. The sergeant brought him to the station house and reported*

him to the superintendent who sent the sergeant home with him. The superintendent brought the case before the provost in the morning at 10 o'clock being the sitting magistrate; he acknowledged his offence and was suspended.

On the night of Thursday the 2nd the superintendent placed Alexander Edgar on duty in the place of Kirkpatrick and on Friday morning the 3rd brought him before the provost he being an applicant for a situation on the force at the police board meeting on Friday the 27th December ultimate – he was sworn in a supernumerary constable."

In 1851 a fresh water supply was introduced to Dumfries. The water was piped from Loch Rutton and to celebrate this, an elaborate ornamental fountain was erected in the High Street in 1887 where it still stands.

On 7th February 1851 James Kirkpatrick aged 60 years of McNaught's Close, Friars Vennel, Dumfries, was dismissed for being found drunk on duty by the superintendent. Alexander Edgar aged 20 years of Friars Vennel, Dumfries, was appointed in his place. William Richardson was found drunk and Francis O'Neil was verbally abusive to Baillie Scott, both were suspended from duty. Richardson was later dismissed and O'Neil reprimanded. John Kennedy was appointed in place of Richardson while supernumerary Constable William McBurnie was advised that his services were no longer required by Superintendent McNabb.

Superintendent McNabb made the following entry in the general order book on 1st March 1851:

"The duty changed Kerr and O'Neal took up day duty Sergt. Richardson, Muir and Edgar night. Richardson No 1 Muir No 2 and Edgar No 3 beats.

By order of Provost Nicholson I gave the men orders when on day duty to prevent public begging in the town and to remove all vagrants from the parish and if they found any of them begging after being removed to bring them to the station that they might be brought before the Magistrate of the week."

On 6th March 1851 Superintendent McNabb completed the following entry in the general order book:

"Police Constable Richardson was reported by Baillie Scott or being drunk at a quarter past 6 o'clock coming off night duty he was reported to Provost Nicholson at the Council Chambers and ordered to be suspended."

In April 1851 Nathan Thomson was appointed, but resigned in August that year through ill health, Thomas McKie was appointed in his place.

In September 1851 Alexander Edgar resigned and Thomas Slimmin appointed. Edgar was unmarried, 20 years of age and stayed in Friars Vennel with his mother.

On March 1st 1852 the station log book records:

"Constables Kerr, Moor and Slimmin took up night duty, Kerr in charge. John McBurnie on duty as supernumerary. Constable O'Neal took up day duty."

A few days later and supernumerary Constable Robert Smith was appointed permanently and put on night duty.

At the police commissioners meeting in March 1852 they discussed a serious fire that had occurred a few days earlier. The commissioners wanted to know if the new hoses they had procured for fighting fires had functioned well.

There was no fire brigade and apparently no volunteers to act as fire fighters. Superintendent McNabb and his watchmen had been called into action and assisted by local people had extinguishing the fire. He reported that the new hoses had functioned well, but that owing to his men being occupied with fighting the fire there had been thefts and looting of property from the premises.

Superintendent McNabb begged the authority to form a fire brigade so that he and his men could deal with policing matters and not devote their time to fighting fires. The commissioners were satisfied with the superintendent's report and agreed that it would:

"...urge upon them the necessity of taking active steps towards its formation."

The meeting appointed Robert Smith in place of Thomas McKie who resigned.

On July 6th 1852 the following entry is noted in the station log book:

"At 10 o'clock p.m. Messrs. Smith and Lawson as members of a committee appointed to enquire into the conduct of the police force visited the police office and examined the charge book and occurrence book and made other enquiries into the working of the police force and went away satisfied and expressed their entire satisfaction with what they had seen and heard.

John Slimmin Sergeant
    Witness: Francis O'Neill Constable

While on 12th April 1852 the station log book reports:

"Constable Donaldson resigned and Maxwell Coats and Nathanial Thomson came on duty as supernumeraries. The Court of Justiciary was held and the police force got new clothing."

On 18th April 1852 the following was published in the 'Standard':

"THEFT AND ESCAPE

On Friday last a large canvas rick-cover was stolen from Marchbank. Two boys, brothers by of the name of McMurdoch, were apprehended on Saturday by the burgh police, charged with offering pieces of the cover for sale to some dealers in old rags. A large portion of the cover was found hidden in a field in the neighbourhood of Marchbank, cut up into pieces for easy transmission. The boys were confined in the low cell at the police office, better known as the "saut box". On Monday morning it was discovered that they had escaped; it is supposed that some confederate had handed them, underneath the door, an instrument to force the bolt of the lock, which could easily be done, and that they thus effected their escape."

On 30th July 1852 Francis O'Neil resigned and John Clint was appointed, while in December that year John Douglas and John Clint were suspended for excessive use of force. Douglas was later dismissed and Clint reprimanded. Shortly after William Anderson, Francis Wilson and Andrew Donaldson were appointed.

Any death in police custody is a tragedy, but the authorities in 1853 didn't have the same attitude as today:

"MEETING OF THE DUMFRIES POLICE COMMISSIONERS 4TH MAY 1853"

".....Superintendent McNabb's report was read. Nothing particular in the discharge of the police duties up till Thursday last, when the man, Edgar, committed suicide in the police office; he was perfectly sober when taken up; no blame could be attached to the police....."

Constable Malcolm Kirkmahoe was appointed in November 1853 and took up night duty with Constables Donaldson, Walsh and supernumerary Constable Armstrong.

On 26th January 1855 Superintendent McNabb was accused of not paying fines monies into the bank. The clerk reported that he was now in arrears amounting to £27:10:8d. It was alleged that he had embezzled public monies. After investigation the committee found that on top of that sum he owed a further 17 shillings and sixpence and another sum of £8:16:00d which had not been paid into the treasurer. Mr. McNabb was suspended from duty and dismissed in disgrace.

As a result of Superintendent McNabb's hasty departure in February 1855, the council ate humble pie and Superintendent Jones of the Dumfries Rural Police was again called into action as the interim Superintendent of Dumfries Burgh.

The 'Standard reports on the Commissioners of Police meeting on 4th April 1855 when they discussed the selection of a new superintendent:

"COMMISSIONERS OF POLICE

…..The meeting then proceeded to the election of a superintendent in room of Mr. McNabb…..Baillie Currie spoke in high terms of Mr. Ingram, who has been nine years in the county force. When he applied to this two months ago his testimonials were so satisfactory that he told Ingram at once – I think you will make a good superintendent and I will vote for you. It was much better to vote for a man like Ingram whom most of them knew, and who was well acquainted with the district, than a stranger. There was not a commissioner present but would say that a better man could scarcely be found. Mr. Ingram wrote a good business hand, would be able to keep their books well; and in regard to his private character, it was of first class. One and all of the Commissioners to whom he had spoken on the subject concurred in saying that both as regards the public and private qualifications of Mr. Ingram, he was well fitted for the situation of their superintendent. He had therefore great pleasure in proposing that he be appointed to the vacant office. Baillie Payne seconded the motion, because of the high testimonials given to Mr. Ingram, and their knowledge of his qualifications. He admired Mr. Jones very much; but they required as a superintendent one who would be every day with them to look after the force.

Baillie Balieff, in proposing Mr. Jones, said he had nothing to say against Mr. Ingram. He was ready to acknowledge his excellent character; but they should bear in mind that a man might be able to act very well as a servant, but not so as a master. In deciding the question before them, they should act as if they were conducting their own business; and certainly if they had five years experience of a servant; and found that he cost them less money and less anxiety, and was in every respect worthy of their trust, they would try to regain that servant rather than take one of whom they had no experience. Some years ago it was well known, the burgh police was in a most disorganized state, and they had applied to Mr. Jones, who soon put it into an efficient condition. Something had been said out of doors regarding the dismission of Mr. Jones, and he wished to refer to his part of the subject for a little. Well then, about two years and a half after Mr. Jones was engaged to act as superintendent, the Commissioners had expressed their sense of the value of his services in the following resolution: 'The Commissioners unanimously express their strong and continued approbation of his conduct since the period of his connection with the police, and order their thanks to be conveyed to him.' With such a resolution as that before him, he thought they would admit that the Commissioners were highly satisfied with their superintendent. It had been argued too, that Mr. Jones's connection with the county unfitted him to superintend the burgh force. This was just one of those ghosts or shadows which are got up when you wish to frighten people. Mr. Jones was superintendent of the burgh police five years, and if in one instance it could be shewn that he had served the county to the detriment of the burgh, or in any respect neglected the interests of the latter, he (Mr. Balieff) would give up his case. This question was one of great importance, and he entreated them to weigh it in all its bearings before coming to a decision. He maintained that during the last two months thefts had been detected which would have been overlooked but for the connection between the county and burgh police. When the force were under different superintendents, jealousies would arise; one man would not tell the other of what was going on because they were under different masters, and thus the police would be less efficient, and the public suffer loss. During the five years of Mr. Jones's service the fines amounted to £224 against £173 imposed during the last five years; and, as regards the expenditure, it was less by about £200 in the first five, as compared with this last five years. Then it was a great thing to have confidence in your superintendent – to have no fear that he would pocket 2 shillings and six pence fine from one man, and 3 shillings of hush money from another. Baillie Balieff concluded by proposing that Mr. Jones be appointed superintendent.

Dean Lawson, in seconding the motion, said he thought they should be very thankful that they had the chance of securing the valuable services of Mr. Jones at such a cheap rate. They would obtain them for £20 or so, a mere nominal sum; whereas if they were compelled by law to appoint such a superintendent, it might cost them £200 per year. It was agreed upon all hands that a better county police than theirs could not be. It stood all thanks to its superintendent; and since they had had the same gentleman for five years, and now had an opportunity of engaging him anew, he thought they should be grateful for the offer. He would not, as on the former occasion, say that the services should be rendered gratuitously, but that a small sum, such as had been mentioned should be given in acknowledgement of them. Mr. Jones too, was a first rate procurator fiscal, and for that reason they should be glad to engage him. He had no ill feeling towards Mr. Ingram, who like himself, was a firm teetotaler; and he was not sorry to see him getting support from certain parties (Laughter) as it shewed that their hostility to teetotalism was on the decline, and that it was making way in public opinion. Mr. Jones, however, was a strictly sober man, and on account of his qualifications well deserved the situation. He attached no greater value to the testimonials read in favour of the other candidate, as certificates equally good had been given in behalf of Mr. McNabb.

Mr. McGowan said Mr. Jones did his work very efficiently, but it had been objected to him that he had interfered with the Magistrates. He would like to know the arrangements regarding salary. If they paid £20 to Mr. Jones, would they have to pay an extra sum to the person under him because of Mr. Jones's inability to be always superintending the force? In that case there might be no saving. In regard to the divided responsibility, of Mr. Jones having to serve both the county and the burgh, he thought that was an objection that could not be got over.

Mr. Sloan said they had proof for five years that Mr. Jones was able to attend to both duties; and that he discharged those relating to the burgh to the same satisfaction of the Commissioners. He had been acting as their superintendent for the last two months, and not a single complaint had been brought against him. A saving was effected of 25 shillings a week and yet the work was efficiently done. Of course if Mr. Jones was appointed, a sergeant would be placed under him; but the salary of the sergeant need not be high, as Mr. Jones was seldom away.

Mr. W. Dickie asked what was the reason that Mr. Jones had not been all along continued as superintendent?

Mr. Balieff thanked Mr. Dickie for putting this question, and then in answer to It stated that a committee had been appointed to look out for a successor to Mr. Waterston (Mr. Jones's sergeant); and one or two of its members, who were magistrates at the time went drunk to the police office - (Hear, hear) – and wished Mr. Jones to receive a false charge, which Mr. Jones refused to do; and they, in revenge, instead of proposing a successor to Mr. Waterston, reported in favour of the commissioners having a superintendent of their own; and in consequence Mr. Jones was parted with. (The Provost: I never heard of the magistrates going drunk to the police office, and don't believe a word of it.) Mr. Balieff, in continuation, said he had stated a fact. It had been told him by Mr. Turner that Mr. Jones had insulted the Magistrates.

Mr. Turner: I only said I had been informed he had acted dictatorially to one of them.

Baillie Payne said that a few days ago Mr. Jones had brought up a little boy before him who had cheated his mother out of 2 shlllings and sixpence, and urged him to send the boy to the jail as it was a case of *theft; but he had nevertheless ruled that it was a breach of trust merely, and had sent the boy to the Ragged School.*

Dean Lawson observed that the superintendent had only been instructing the magistrate in his duty, Baillie Payne considered Mr. Jones had been ignorant of his duty in the case under consideration. Baillie Balieff had been told by the Magistrates repeatedly, and he had found it so by his own experience, that a more civil, obliging and attentive office than Mr. Jones could not exist.

After some more discussion the vote was taken when twelve votes for Mr. Ingram, and eleven for Mr. Jones. Mr. Ingram was thus elected by a majority of one….. Neither of the other candidates was proposed.

It was then resolved, on the motion of Baillie Payne, to present Mr. Jones with £10, in acknowledgement of his two months services as superintendent. – The Provost also moved a vote of thanks to Mr. Jones. He had always found him civil and attentive, and had no objection to him; but he wanted a man whose whole services the Commissiomners could command. – Baillie Currie, in seconding the vote of thanks, corroborated the statements of the Provost.- Baillie Balieff considered that in justice to Mr. Jones, these testimonies should have been made before the vote was taken.

The committee appointed to investigate into the nature and extent of Mr. McNabb's defalcations, reported them to amount to £81 and 10 shillings, but stated, that as they were not lawyers, they could not give any opinion as to who was liable. A letter was read from Mr. Young, the county fiscal, in answer to the question put to him as to whether the ex-superintendent could be prosecuted criminally, - Mr. Young stated that he could not answer that question until a direct charge of fraud or swindling had been made against Mr. McNabb, instead, simply of accusations of a deficiency. - A committee was then named to wait upon Mr. Young to make up his opinion."

Chapter Five
SUPERINTENDENT GEORGE INGRAM

At a meeting of the Police Commissioners for Dumfries Burgh on 4th April 1855 a replacement for McNabb was sought. There were three candidates, John Haining, Alexander Cooper and George Ingram. Ingram was a veteran of nine years police service with the Dumfries County Police at Langholm. A faction of the council still wanted Mr. Jones to continue as superintendent, but others wanted their own superintendent of police.

During debate the choice came down to two men, John Jones who, incidentally had not even applied for the post, and George Ingram.

Ingram was a native of Daviot, Aberdeen, was married to Mary Irvine and was 26 years of age. He was the son of George Ingram, a farmer, and his wife Janet Ingram. At the time of his appointment he was the constable at Langholm in the Dumfriesshire County Police.

As a mark of their gratitude the council also voted to pay Mr. Jones the sum of £10 for acting as interim superintendent for the previous two months.

"BURGH POLICE COURT, DUMFRIES April 21st 1856

Public House Cases Tried Before Baillie Balieff

Case against Mathew Robertson

Mathew Robertson, grocer and spirit dealer, Queensberry Street, was charged at the instance of George Ingram, superintendent of police, with breach of certificate, by selling, on the 31st March, one pint of ale to be consumed on the premises. R. Houston, supernumerary police officer, deponed that on the 31st March he went to Robertson's shop and asked for a pint of ale, when he was shown into the back shop and supplied with the ale by a woman who he supposed to be Robertson's wife. Saw another person named Kerr in the back shop drinking ale. Does not remember what day of the week was the 31st march: thought it was a Wednesday. The witness, who was rather confused in giving his evidence, was subjected to a long cross examination by Mr. J.A. Smyth, with a view to shewing that he was unworthy of credit. Had been in the employment of the Crichton Institution before engaging in the police, but he declined saying why he had left it. On the same day he was at

Robertson's had gone to Hellon's and bought a gill of whisky, which he took to the police office, where it was drunk. He had been ordered by the superintendent to go to the public house; had paid the money from his own pocket; expected to be repaid for it, but had no promise of receiving any portion of any fines.. Baillie Balieff said that the man Kerr should have been produced as a witness. He though that when than more witness could be adduced that they should be brought forward. He was not inclined to find the case proven on the evidence of a witness who was so confused as Houston, who he believed was innocent of anything beyond giving his evidence confusedly, caused by the manner he had been treated by Mr. Smyth. He considered it quite right for the police to endeavour to detect persons breaking the law; if they endeavoured to entrap and coax people to break the law, they would be to blame; but if they went, in the casual way, and asked for a drink, he thought they were doing what was right, in order to punish those who broke the law. From the loose manner the witness gave his evidence he must hold the case not proven."

"Case against William Dryden

William Dryden, Anchor Inn, was accused of breach of certificate, by keeping open house on the Sabbath the 6th instant. Robert Houston, constable, deponed that on the day he went to Dryden's house and asked for a glass of ale; got it from Mrs. Dryden. – Cross examined by Mr. T.H. McGowan – I Went to Dryden's by Mr. Ingram's orders; he did not mention Dryden, but told me to go and try the public houses. I Began at the 'Sands; went into two or three houses there, and went to others. I was about two hours going among them. I Did not get ale in them all and had four glasses altogether. I Paid 1.5 pennies per glass, except at Dryden's, where 2 pennies was charged. At Mrs. Hunter's I was refused ale – when a baker who was in the house, and knew me formally, said she might give it which she did. Did not say I came from the country, and was not a traveller. At Hellon's I asked when the train started. Hellon said half past seven. He might have believed I was going by railway from my asking the question, but I did not say so. The money expended on ale I expect to be repaid by Mr. Ingram; but no promise was made of getting a part of the penalties. I was engaged about three weeks ago. Was told I would have to go to public houses. I had on my ordinary clothes. I have been on night duty since I entered the police, and usually wear my own clothes when off duty. I have been at Dryden's house before when living in the country. George Ingram, superintendent of police, examined by Mr. McGowan; I engaged Houston as a supernumerary. I told him he would have to go to public houses, but did not say that it was part of his duty. I sent him to public houses on my own authority. I told Houston his expenses would be paid by myself. Houston has no promise of any portion of fines that may be recovered. The Town Clerk does not prepare the complaints, nor revise

them. He is paid the fees prescribed; if the cases fail he is entitled to his
fees if he demands them. He has not asked for the fees in such cases.
I do not pay the officer; that is done by the clerk – Mr. Martin, Town
Clerk explained that the magistrates would sign no warrant unless it
passed through the hands of the Town Clerk, and he merely affixed his
initials for that purpose. William Wilson, burgh officer, deponed he
served the summons; in such cases he had not asked for his fee when the
case had failed. Mr. McGowan held that the case had not been proven;
and strongly condemned the conduct of the superintendent in resorting
to what he described as a spy system, in order to punish violations
of the Public House Act. Mr. Ingram maintained that the case was
clearly proven, and that Mr. McGowan not adducing the evidence of the
defender' wife and other persons to prove that no ale had been served
sold showed that the witness, Houston, was correct. Baillie Balieff
said that if this case had come before him first he would have found it
proven, but from the witness's confused manner in the former case he
would give the defender the benefit of the doubt, and find the case not
proven. Mr. McGowan claimed expenses, but the magistrate refused."

Mr. Ingram was not to be beaten and shortly thereafter ale house licence
holder William Bryden was again in the dock:

"PUBLIC HOUSE CASE DUMFRIES

On Saturday last, a complaint was preferred before Baillie Pagan, at the
instance of Superintendent Ingram, against William Dryden, Anchor
Inn, for breach of certificate by selling liquor after eleven o clock at night
on Tuesday 7th instant. Helen Fitzimmons or Coil deponed that on the
night in question she had purchased a gill and a half of whisky from the
defender's wife; but on going home found, that by mistake, there was
only one gill; she returned and received the half gill from Mrs. Dryden.
On going out she was stopped by a policeman who examined the bottle:
could not say what o'clock it was when she went first; but all the shops
were shut; she was sure it did not exceed fifteen minutes from the time
she got the gill that she returned and got the half gill. Thomas Wilson,
police officer, deponed that on ascertaining what the previous witness
had, he went and charged Mrs. Dryden with selling drink at improper
hours. She at first denied having done so, but afterwards admitted the
facts, and offered him half a crown not to give information, which he
refused to accept. When he saw the woman coming he looked at the
midsteeple clock (the clock is illuminated) and found that it was about
five minutes past 12. The witness was cross examined by Mr. T.H.
McGowan, with a view to illicit whether he and another policeman had
a short time ago, gone into the defenders house after 12 0'clock at night
and demanded a bottle of portal which was given them. The witness
declined to answer the question as not being connected with the case
before the court, upon which, Mr. McGowan, intimated that he would

prefer a complaint to the police commissioners against the witness with a view of having them dismissed from the force.

Mrs. Dryden, on being examined, acknowledged that she had sold the liquor, but it was two minutes to 11 o'clock when the woman got it. She came back about twenty minutes or half an hour later and she admitted that she had offered the policeman half a crown to say nothing of the matter. Helen Dryden, daughter of the preceding witness, swore that the drink was given two minutes before 11 o'clock and that the woman returned within half an hour. Mr. Ingram addressed the court, and maintained that the complaint had been proved. Mr. McGowan, on the other hand, contended that there was no proof that the liquor was supplied after 11 o'clock. Baillie Pagan said that the whisky given the second time being to rectify a mistake, it might be passed over, and in regard to the first time at which the woman received the liquor she could not speak distinctly, while the officer gave no evidence on that point. On the other hand, Mrs. Dryden and her daughter had sworn that it was sold two minutes before eleven. He did not think that there was anything singular in these witnesses looking at the clock at a particular time, as he considered it was the duty of publicans when near the hour, to ascertain whether or not they could lawfully supply liquor to any person not residing in the house. He thought that the evidence had failed to shew that the liquor had been supplied after eleven o'clock, and therefore found the complaint not proven."

In June 1856 the 'Standard' reported the following harrowing tale:

"ALLEGED MANSLAUGHTER OF A LUNATIC

At the Bow Street police court on Monday, Mr. Charles Snape resident surgeon at the county lunatic asylum at Wandsworth, was summoned by the commissioners in lunacy, to answer a charge of having killed Daniel Dolley, aged 65 years, an inmate of that establishment. The surgeon had ordered the deceased to have a cold shower – bath in which he was kept twenty eight minutes and fifteen or sixteen minutes after he was taken out he died. It was calculated that there must have been 600 gallons of cold water poured down upon the head of the deceased while in the bath. A post mortem examination of the body was afterwards made by Mr. Snape and his colleagues, the examination being conducted by a young man who had just passed the college of surgeons, and a verdict of 'natural death' was recorded. Some witnesses were examined in support of the charge, after which the case was adjourned for two or three weeks, for the convenience of counsel. The defendant, who had appeared by summons, was not required to give bail for his future attendance."

"CASE OF THOMAS JOHNSTON

23rd April 1856

At the recent Newcastle assizes, Thomas Johnston, tailor, Dumfries, was tried on a charge of having committed rape at Haltwhistle in April 1853, found guilty, and sentenced to transportation for life. As he was in very poor circumstances, only two witnesses for his defence could be provided; and it is believed by those who knew the case, that owing to this and other unfortunate circumstances, he did not get a fair trial; and also that he is really guiltless of the crime for which he is now in prison. A memorial to the Queen, accompanied with some depositions of numerous witnesses in his behalf, some of whom were not available till after the trial, have been forwarded to our burgh member, and by him taken to the Home Office for presentation to her Majesty. Robert Muir Esq. writer, here, has in the most liberal manner taken charge of the proceedings, and been at no small pains to collect the evidence and get it put into a proper shape; his only fee in the case being the heart satisfaction of trying to rescue from the fangs of the law a fellow creature who he believes to have been wrongously convicted. A small fund has been raised here to defray the necessary outlay incurred in the matter, though it is still far from sufficient for the purpose, and additions to it would be highly acceptable. It remains to be seen whether the application that has been made for a royal pardon to Johnston, for the reasons stated in the depositions and memorial, will be attended with success."

Further enquiry into what became of Thomas Johnston revealed that:

The Edwin Fox was an 892 ton ship built in Calcutta in 1853. It was used for transporting convicts from the UK to Western Australia and left Plymouth on August 26th 1858 bound for Swan River Colony. She carried the 21st of 37 shipments of male convicts destined for Western Australia. Among the convicts was:

"Thomas Johnston. Convict No 5328, aged 46 years, sentenced to 10 years at Newcastle Assizes in 1856 for the carnal knowledge of a girl under ten years."

The Police (Scotland) Act 1857 (20 & 21 Vict. c.72), one of the Police (Scotland) Acts 1857 to 1890. The legislation made the establishment of a police force mandatory in the counties of Scotland and allowed existing burgh police forces to be consolidated with a county force although this was not adopted locally and the Dumfries Burgh Police remained independent of the Dumfries County Police.

In June 1856 the following was reported in the 'Standard':

"THE SISTER OF BURNS

The sister of Burns still lives at Bridgehouse on the Doon at the age of eighty four, supported mainly by the proceeds of a subscription which was raised for her about fourteen years ago. Her daughters, Agnes and Isabella Begg, whose heroic exertions for her support through many years of neglect drew forth much praise, continue to live with her unmarried. Seeing that the greater part of Mrs. Begg's income would die with her, Messrs Chambers published in a cheap form a few years ago an edition of Mr. R Chambers' "Life and Works of Burns", and requested a special favour of the booksellers in promoting its sale, as the profits were to be given to a fund whereby a provision for the nieces of Burns might be completed after their mothers death. The object was the most interesting as Mrs. Begg regarded the scheme as taking the last load of earthly care off her mind. The public and the 'trade' will be gratified to learn that £200 had been lately handed to the Misses Begg, accumulated at the interest till the close of Mrs. Begg's life – when with another sum remaining from the subscription, it will be sunk in annuities on the lives of the Misses Begg, who already enjoy life pensions of £10 each from the government, granted them by Sir Robert Peel. Thus, what with the public beneficence and what their own industry, the permanent comfort of those interesting relatives of the Scottish poet may be considered as secured."

On 25th March 1857 the burgh council held their monthly meeting:

"THE SUPERINTENDENT'S REPORT

The Superintendent's (monthly) report was then produced. He states that the town generally had been in a quiet state. There had been:

Cases of assault:	*19;*
Breach of the peace:	*4;*
Breach of certificate:	*2;*
Chimneys on fire:	*7*
Drunk and disorderly:	*13*
Drunk and incapable:	*20*
Malicious mischief:	*3*
Reset of theft:	*2*
Selling spirits without a certificate	*1*
Theft:	*14*
Total cases:	*85*
Corresponding month last year:	*83*

Thefts reported where apprehensions and recoveries were effected: 6
Value of property: £6: 3 shillings and 9 pence

Thefts where neither apprehensions nor recoveries were effected: 4
Value of property: £2: 0 shillings and 6 pence

Fines recovered: £15: 13 shillings
Fines unrecovered   £5
Total fines £15: 18 shillings
Total fines in corresponding month last year: £11

After the report had been read the meeting was adjourned."

The problem with controlling liquor licensing was an almost weekly issue for the burgh police and the Dumfries and Galloway Standard reports in June 1857:

"Dumfries Burgh Police Court

On Thursday Joseph Hellon, grocer and spirit dealer, English Street, James Lumsden, grocer and spirit dealer St Michael Street, and John Black, grocer and spirit dealer English Street appeared before Baillie Currie at the instance of George Ingram, superintendent of police, charged with breach of their certificates. Hellon with having sold one gill or other quantity of whisky before 6 o'clock on the morning of the 1st current, and black and Lumsden, which having each sold one pint or other quantity of ale to be drunk or consumed on the premises on the 31st ult. The Baillie having hearing evidence, found the complaints proven against Hellon and Lumsden qnd fined Lumsden £1 5 shillings and expenses. But as the case against Hellon was a narrow one, the Baillie thought the ends of justice would be satisfied by him paying the expenses, to which Hellon readily agreed. From the contradictory nature of the evidence in Black's case, the Baillie found it not proven."

The ordinary monthly meeting of the Commissioners of Police was reported in the 'Standard' and Superintendent Ingram's unpopularity with the Commissioners of Police is evident:

"Superintendent Ingram's report for May was read. The Town, he says, has been in a turbulent state during the past month; and he specifies one case of crime, happily or rare occurrence in the district, an assault by stabbing committed upon Robert McAdam, ostler, Dumfries, on the night of the 26th inst., by John Miller, a railway labourer, from Edinburgh, who was apprehended, and is now undergoing a period of 60 days imprisonment with hard labour, for the crime...... Mr. Ingram also reported that Constable Robert Kerr, was on the 20th inst. reported by him to Baillie Waugh; the sitting magistrate, for being drunk and

unfit for duty at a quarter to four o'clock on the morning of that day, and for calling him, the superintendent, a number of approbrious and profane epithets (specified in the report) , when Kerr was checked by him in the police office for being drunk. Kerr was stated also to have been the worse of drink when coming off duty at six o'clock on the morning of the 6th inst. Kerr denied all the charges; but the Baillie, after hearing evidence, found them proven, and suspended him till this day's meeting of the Commission.

The case led to a great deal of discussion – Baillie Mundell expressing a desire to hear the exculpatory evidence in it, and stating that it would be unfair to condemn Kerr merely on the evidence of two policemen – Dean Blaind was of a similar opinion and considered that Kerr might had been led to use the improper language attributed to him by being incensed on account of being subject of a false charge. Dr. McCulloch condemned the practice which appeared to him to be prevalent of depreciating the police officers and representing them as unworthy to be believed. He could not see what other evidence they were likely to have in many cases at four o'clock in the morning, nor could he imagine more trustworthy evidence that that given by their most respectable superintendent. He referred to the antecedents of Kerr as affording a strong presumption of the truth of the present charge; and, in regard to the abusive language laid to this charge; averred that a majority of the Commissioners had, by their decisions and otherwise, given hint to the officers that they might abuse the Superintendent as they pleased, him being a marked man. Baillie Mundell hoped that nothing that had fallen from Dr. McCulloch would lend the Commissioners or the public to think that he wished to set aside the evidence against the accused; all he wished was to hear both sides of the case. – Mr. McGowan thought it was very clear, after the warning given to Kerr and the repeated charges against him, that he was too long in the force, and ought to be got rid of.

The discussion was continued; a somewhat amusing one, being occassionallyt mixed up with it, for the purpose of determining what effect one of two glasses of which will have on a man, or at what stage of drinking may be called drunk. Eventually, Mr. Brown seconded by Mr. McGowan, moved that Kerr be dismissed; and Baillie Mundell, seconded by Dean Blaind; proposed, as an amendment, that the witnesses in the case be examined by the Commission before deciding in it. The amendment was carried by a majority of 13 to 5..... Kerr, being brought in denied having been drunk; but admitted that on the charge being made against him by the superintendent he had said it was a 'damned lie'. He had only got one glass of whisky that morning. A note from his landlady, Mrs. Davidson, was produced in which she stated that, when admitted by her at four o'clock on the Thursday morning, he was perfectly sober – so far as she was able to judge. A young woman living in Wilson's Close stated that Kerr had come down the close that morning between 2 and 3 o'clock he having been led to do so by hearing her mother who was then on her death bed, moaning loudly, When Kerr spoke to the witness, the window was between them; he seemed to be quite sober, and her sister looked after him as he went up the close, and did not think he was the worse of drink. James Thom, a scavenger, saw Kerr going home about 4 o'clock on Thursday morning, when he appeared to be walking steadily enough. Baillie Mundell said that he had occasion to go to his shop for some documents at one o'clock that morning; he spoke with Kerr then and at that time he seemed perfectly sober.

Superintendent Ingram and Constables Wilson and Welsh then severally gave their evidence, which was in effect that Kerr was so much the worse of liquor at the time specified that he could not stand without swaggering, or speak without stammering; and that on calmly being charged with the offence by the Superintendent, he had assailed the Superintendent with a number of epithets, which we do not care about repeating. The evidence of a baker, named Dickson, who said he saw Kerr when going home splaiting his legs; and that of a supernumerary policeman named Templeton, who declared that Kerr was that morning as drunk a man as ever he saw able to walk.

Mr. Brown repeated his motion to dismiss Kerr from the force – seconded by Mr. McGowan, and agreed to unanimously....."

In 1857 the council lease on the watch house at the Midsteeple in High Street was due for renewal and the owner of the property, David Milligan, the flesher, asked for the premises to be returned to him. The council began to look for a new police office, but set aside David Milligan's request until they could find suitable premises.

In June 1857 Mr. Ingram was called before the commissioners charged with:

".....compromising certain publican's cases on payment of certain sums of money, without the offending parties having been brought publicly before the court."

Effectively the superintendent, who was also Inspector of Weights and Measures and Inspector of Ale Certificates, was accused of accepting payment from publicans in lieu of reporting them to the court in his other capacity as the Procurator Fiscal for the Burgh Justices of the Peace.

After two meetings of the commissioners a committee of five was set up to investigate the superintendent's actions. Mr. Ingram intimated that he reported these cases as an individual and not as superintendent or procurator fiscal and that the expenses of these cases came from his own pocket and not the councils, therefore the arrangements he came to with the publicans and inn keepers was the same as his predecessors, including Mr. Jones and a portion of the money was paid into the poor house.

During this period there was also a complaint from the constables regarding Mr. Ingram's conduct. He had been given a £1 by the council for extra duties during elections. The constables were unhappy that he divided 7 shillings and sixpence among them and kept the remaining 12 shillings and sixpence for himself. After enquiry the councilors dismissed the complaint.

The whole unseemly affair was finally resolved in July 1858 when Superintendent Ingram resigned upon his appointment as Superintendent of Police at Paisley.

Mr. Ingram died on 21st October 1871 aged 48 years, of typhus fever, whilst still superintendent of Paisley burgh police. He was survived by his wife, Mary and eight children.

During February / March 1858 the council purchased a shop in Queensberry Street and immediately there was outcry from their new neighbours, as they thought there would be too much noise. The ground floor was completely changed to accommodate the police. The new office was completed on 29th May 1858 and the Midsteeple office was returned to its owner.

There has been confusion over the years as to where this police office was actually located; as the burgh records recount the purchase of the shop in Queensberry Street, but fail to give a number or location. The street numbering and alignment of Queensberry Street has changed over the years so the modern numbering cannot be relied upon. From enquiry the location appears to be to the south of the Ewe and Lamb Close (which was later widened and became Munches Street). It was also near to Dickson's Close, which no longer exists but would have been approximately where the present day Solicitors Property Centre is situated, and it was also adjacent to Old Union Street. The location is further mentioned in the 1861 Census which shows that:

"No persons slept in the police office on the night of Sunday April 7th 1861".

The address given against this entry; shows that the premises was in the south west side of Queensberry Street, between Union Street and High Street, but no street number is shown against the entry. Further enquiry shows that there were two shops under the tollbooth building and this leads to the belief that the police office, which consisted of two rooms, was situated within one of these two shops under the tollbooth in Queensberry Street.

The 'Standard', on 24th August 1858 reported on the Commissioners of Police meeting to appoint the new superintendent:

"COMMISSIONERS OF POLICE

A special meeting of this body was held yesterday..... The Provost stated the object of the meeting was to consider the applications made for the office of superintendent of the police force. These applications, 30 in number, with accompanying testimonials, were read – a process which occupied fully an hour. On the motion of Baillie Waugh, seconded by Mr. McGowan, it was agreed to reduce the candidates to a leet of seven – an amendment of Dean Blaind, to defer further proceedings till the regular meeting on Friday, not having been seconded.

The following seven candidates obtained the greatest number of votes:-

Mr. D. Anderson, Inverness: 13
Mr. B. Dickson, Lerwick: 12
Mr. W. Mitchell, Dumfries: 11 votes
Mr. A Hunter, Bakewell: 9
Mr. W.J. Paterson, Kirkcudbright: 9
Mr. B. Saggerson, Oldham: 9 and
Mr. R. Strong, Liverpool: 7.

The meeting then adjourned till the 27th instant, when we suppose, the election will be proceeded with."

The committee met again on 27th August and appointed David Anderson from Inverness as the new superintendent of burgh police.

Chapter Six
SUPERINTENDENT DAVID ANDERSON

The next Superintendent of Burgh Police was to be David Anderson aged 37 years, born at Inverness in1821, the son of John Anderson, a linen weaver and Agnes Myles or Anderson. Mr. Anderson was married man with four sons. He was appointed superintendent of burgh police on 27th August 1858.

Inverness burgh police records show that David Anderson was the first Superintendent of Inverness burgh police; he was appointed on 4 September 1847 and remained in post until 3rd May 1854 when he left to become a burgh and criminal officer in Inverness.

On 29th September 1858 the commissioners met again:

"DUMFRIES POLICE COMMISSIONERS

The September meeting of this Board was held yesterday in the Council Chambers.....Baillie Waugh stated that a supernumerary constable, named Peter Campbell, had been reported to him as having been intoxicated on duty, and he had suspended him. He had now to move that this suspension be ratified, and that the superintendent be instructed to fill up the vacancy – agreed to.

Baillie Waugh also moved that an allowance of 15 shillings each be made to constables Wilson and Smith, who had conducted the police affairs with great efficiency during the ten or twelve days of interval between the departure of Superintendent Ingram, and the arrival of Superintendent Anderson."

There was also a motion at this meeting to increase the wages of the constables from 15 shillings a week to 18 shillings a week and this was widely supported, but a motion was carried to include this in the remit of the new superintendent to report back to the commissioners with his recommendation.

Superintendent Anderson submitted his first report to the Commissioners of Police meeting on 29th October 1858:

"DUMFRIES POLICE COMMISSIONERS

The monthly meeting of this Board was held yesterday in the Council Chambers......The Clerk read the following report by the Superintendent.

' to report upon the police force, its efficiency and working, whether any addition should be made to its members, and to include the question of wages.'

On that remit the superintendent begs respectfully to report that the police force is not efficient, nor, in his opinion will it be as until the number of men is augmented. The men at present under him he has found diligent and anxious in the discharge of their duty, and he has had no cause of complaint against any one of them. The wages of the policemen he considers too low, and he suggests – 1st. the addition of three extra men, two for night and one for day duty. The arrangement as to pay, &c., he suggests should be thus:- 1 night sergeant, wages 20 shillings; one overseer of scavengers and inspector of nuisances, 19 shillings; 7 constables (2 during day and 5 during night), each at 17 shillings, with 6 pence each additional per week in lieu of boots, thus placing them on the same footing as the county force. He proposes further that 1 shilling per week should be retained from each until the Commissioners shall have in their hands 14 days full pay. This suggestion is made with the view of securing the return of clothing and other articles supplied, in case of resignation or dismissal. In the latter case the Commissioners should reserve power to forfeit back pay. The Superintendent has since he took duty, introduced the use of lamps for the use of the night officers, and signal whistles – the use has already proved beneficial. He hopes the Commissioners will approve of this arrangement. He suggests that the men be supplied with waterproof capes, those in present in use being worthless. He has examined the fire hose and engines. The latter is almost useless from long neglect, the machinery being clagged and rusty, and totally unfit for effectual service. They are now in course of being cleaned and put in proper order, and though not much required within the burgh, he deemed it proper to have the engines put in proper working order. The hose is in tolerable condition; though pretty well worn, they require only to be kept soft and pliable by proper greasing regularly applied, and which is now in course of being done. He begs to state that the quantity of hose is too small, and would therefore suggest that an additional quantity of leather copper-riveted hose should be made to the present stock. The wheel barrow presently used for conveying the hose he suggest should be kept close to the police office, so that in cases of fire the hose may be made available the moment an alarm of fire is given. The fire engines require painting, which is now being done at his suggestion, and by order of the sitting magistrate. The Superintendent begs next to report that there are 201 brokers shops (Wee pawns), or dealers in second hand goods, in Dumfries, none of whom are licensed or keep books, as is required by the Act of Parliament. To remedy this defect, he suggests the immediate enforcement of the Act of Parliament, requiring them to register their names and keep a book same as that herewith produced, which he has obtained from Glasgow, and which he now submits for your inspection

and approval. No broker should be registered unless he possess one of these books. He has surveyed the common lodging-houses: they are 34 in number with 150 beds available for lodgers; some of them ought to be suppressed, and others limited as to sleeping accommodation; and he submits that the sooner means are adopted to enforce the regulations the better. Very few nuisances exist – there are some, however, and they are now in course of being dealt with. He suggests the introduction of gas to the privy in the close opposite the police office. During the month from the 23rd Sept. to the 27th. inst., 124 persons have been apprehended for crime. Of these, 63 reside within the burgh, and 61 elsewhere. Fines were imposed to the amount of £28 12 shillings, and the sums recovered amount to £22 14 shillings and six pence. The greatest cause of annoyance has been the great influx of cardsharpers, pickpockets, and others of that class during the Rood Fair and Games. 4 watches were snatched from the person; 3 of which were recovered, and the thieves apprehended. Small sums of money were also lost. Cases of drunkenness and disorderly conduct have been numerous; but nearly one half of those taken into custody were not residenters in Dumfries.
The Provost remarked that the addition to the police force recommended in the report would require and outlay of about £200 yearly. Treasurer Nicholson thought it would be advisable to delay the consideration of the report until the new board came into office. He moved accordingly. Mr. Turner seconded the motion. Mr. Bendall, seconded by Mr. Corson, moved that the report be taken up just now. On a division, the motion for delay was carried by 12 votes to 7 votes.....

The report of the committee on the new police office stated that after inspecting plans submitted by Mr. Fraser, the committee had approved of them, and resolved to invite tenders from contractors for the masonry and wood work."

Even though his reign was to be relatively short, Superintendent Anderson had the usual issues to deal with.

Licensing of ale houses and hotels had been an issue for all his predecessors and he was to face the same. The licensing court reports as follows:

"On November 2nd 1858 the half yearly statutory courts for the burgh of Dumfries was held within the council chambers; present were Provost Leighton and Baillies Pagan, Mundell and Waugh.

James Dickson, Queensberry Street, applied for a certificate for an inn for the premises formerly known as the Cross Keys Inn. The clerk stated that this was a new application; the certificate had been withdrawn at the last court in the spring. He then read a testimonial as to Dickson's good character and fitness to keep an inn, to which was appended the names of a number of persons in Dumfries and neighbourhood, including the Reverend Alexander Brown, Free church, Ruthwell. The clerk stated that all the names were written in the same hand, and were not signatures. Baillie Pagan said that at the last licensing court the certificate had been unanimously refused, owing to the irregular character of the house and its being frequented by prostitutes. The disorders in the house had come under the cogniscence of the police court; a very violent assault had been committed in the house, the police found in the room three prostitutes and three men, but the case was not of a nature to be described. The landlady was warned that if she persisted in harbouring such characters the certificate would be taken away; but notwithstanding that caution, within two days thereafter the police found the same three prostitutes in the house. He knew nothing of the conduct or character of the occupant of the Cross Keys accept what had come before him as a magistrate, and the case was so strong that the withdrawal of the licence was unanimously agreed to. He knew of no reason to justify them in again granting a certificate and he moved that this application be refused.

In answer to a question by the provost, Mr. T.F. Smith, writer (a lawyer), who appeared for the applicant, stated that he knew many of the persons whose names were adhibited had given authority to do so.

Provost Leighton doubted the correctness of the report of the police; he did not believe a fourth of it was true.

Baillie Pagan said evidence had been brought before him in the police court that the house was frequented by prostitutes, and was conducted contrary to the terms of the certificate.

Provost Leighton said the landlord could not prevent prostitutes standing in the close. He was informed by Mr. McGeorge, their late fiscal, that the girls were merely standing in the close and not in the house. The clerk stated that the charge was that the girls were not standing in a close, but in the house.

Baillie Pagan repeated his statement that it was proved before him that the police found three prostitutes in this house on two occasions.

Baillie Mundell aid that Baillie Pagan's statement made at the last court was not denied there, and he saw no cause again to grant the certificate.

Provost Leighton said that these girls must go somewhere to get a glass when they wanted it. They had as good a right as themselves to go and get a drink when they chose.

The clerk said that this was against the terms of the certificate to serve such persons with liquor.

Provost Leighton said, People are not to know what kind of girls they are when they go to a dram shop; and it was probable that Dickson and his wife did not know the character of these women. He believed that Dickson's father in law was a respectable man. The clerk stated that he was.

Baillie Pagan did not know anything of the parties except from what he learned in his magisterial capacity. Mr. Smith said he was given to understand that the circumstances which came before the last court could have been explained. Baillie Pagan stated that the facts came out as evidence and could not be denied. Baillie Mundell said that Baillie Pagan, as a magistrate, was cognicent of the facts, and they could not get over these.

The provost thought that these were exaggerated.

Baillie Pagan asked the clerk if the facts were as stated. The clerk stated that, there was not a doubt as to the facts. Baillie Waugh could not agree to grant a certificate.

The certificate was refused three to one."

In another case before Sheriff Trotter, the superintendent gave his evidence:

"SHERIFF CRIMINAL COURT

14th October 1858

Before Sheriff Substitute Trotter

Thomas Nathanial Thomson, a labourer, was charged with stealing from James Patterson, cattle jobber, Caldowbridge, parish of Balmaclellan, while in the Black Bull Inn, Brewery Street, Dumfries on 16th September last, a bank note for £20. Panel pled not guilty, and a jury was empanelled to try the case.

James Patterson, cattle jobber examined: I attended a cattle market here on the 15th September last. I presented a draft for £42 at the Clydesdale Bank, on the 16th and received two £20 notes and two 20 shilling notes. I placed the notes in my pocket book and went to the Black Bull Inn, where I bought a pony, and sent out to get change for one of the £20 notes to pay for it. I laid my pocket book down on the table, and read a letter. I had been getting a glass or two, but was not intoxicated. There were two men sitting there. [Identifies the prisoner as one of them] After I had read the letter, the servant came and asked me if I had all my money. I looked the pocket book, and found there was £20 note gone. Prisoner had gone out the room by that time. The other man was there, but he was asleep. A policeman was sent for, and got information of the circumstances. I saw the £20 note the next day in the Fiscal's office [Identifies it].

Cross examined by Mr. Martin for the panel: I purchased the pony from Thomas Flynn. I paid £40 for it. I will swear that I did not toss for five-half mutchkins in the Black Bull that afternoon. I did not throw my money about the floor.

Catherine Johnstone, daughter of Wm. Johnstone, keeper of the Black Bull: I remember Mr. Patterson being in my father's public house on the 16th Sept. I saw he had two £20 notes, one of which he gave to Hugh Lancaster and Thomas Flynn to get changed. He laid the other down on the table among letters and papers. Patterson was very tipsy. I noticed Thomson, the prisoner, left some of Patterson's papers off the floor, and lay them on the table, and then he sat down beside Patterson. The latter was reading a letter. After Thomson lifted the papers, I saw he had a bank note in his hand, looking at it. I took the note out of his hand and laid it on the table, telling Patterson to put up his money. I then went to sweep the floor. After a little, I saw the prisoner go out, and then I went to the bundle of papers on the table and looked if the note was among them. It was not there, not in the pocket book. A policeman was then sent for, and I heard afterwards that he had captured Thomson with the note in his possession. Before Thomson went out of the house, Patterson had said that he had lost his money. Thomson thereupon rose, and with an oath, asked if he thought he had his note. With that he went out.

Agnes Johnstone, niece of William Johnstone, was the next witness. His evidence did not vary from that of the preceding.

Thomas Flynn, general dealer, Dumfries; I sold a pony to Mr. Patterson at the Black Bull on 16th September. He gave me a £20 note to change, and when I came back I missed the prisoner, who had been there when I left. Patterson was rather fresh with drink, but quite sensible of what he was doing. He complained of having lost a £20 note when I came back.

Andrew Leslie, labourer, Maxwelltown: I was in the Black Bull on 16th September, and I heard the servant tell Thomson to give Mr. Patterson his money. Prisoner said to Patterson, "Do you think I would take your bloody note".

Cross examined by Mr. Martin: I saw the prisoner restore a note to Mr. Patterson twice that afternoon. The note had been lying on the table, and the prisoner lifted it twice, and handed it to Patterson.

John McLure, shoemaker, English Street, Dumfries: on the 16th September, between six and seven o'clock in the evening, I was standing in my own door, when the prisoner came up and asked if I had and change.

John Wylie Hinter: I remember the prisoner coming to the shop which I take charge of in English Street, and ask for change of a £20 note. I directed him to the baker's as a likely place to get change.

Cross examined by Mr. Martin: My first impression was that he asked me where he could get a piece of money deposited.

John Moor, police officer: I captured the prisoner on the 16th September, about 7 o'clock, at Nith Place. I told him he was charged with stealing a £20 note from the Black Bull, but he denied having any note. When I took him to the police office he handed out a note [identifies it] to the superintendent. He said it belonged to a drunken farmer.

David Anderson, police superintendent: When the prisoner came to the office, he said that he had taken the note from a drunken farmer at the Black Bull, who was throwing his money around carelessly about him. Prisoner told me he had taken the note merely to take care of it. Afterwards he said the farmer had given it to him.

The prisoner's declaration was then read: It bore that he was 43 years of age, and had no fixed place of residence. On the 16th September he was in the Black Bull, where he saw the farmer, who was tipsy, with his money strewn about. A £20 note fell, and he lifted it and placed it in the farmer's hand. This occurred three times. He then said to the farmer that he was sorry to see him in that state and he would keep the note until he was better able to take care of it. Prisoner took a stroll, and was apprehended by a police officer. Prisoner disclaimed any intention of keeping the note.

The jury, after a few minutes consultation, found the panel guilty as libeled. Mr. Martin put in two certificates of character. The Sheriff, in consideration of the temptation offered to the prisoner, passed a mitigated sentence of three months imprisonment."

Superintendent Anderson, aged 37 years (not about 45 years as reported in the press) was born at Inverness in1821 unfortunately died in office in June 1859 after a long illness. His cause of death was described as, 'Discane of the Brain.' Superintendent Anderson was married to Ann Martin or Anderson and they had four sons, the eldest of which, John Anderson, completed his father's death certificate.

Superintendent Anderson was interred at St. Mary's Church Dumfries and the Dumfries and Galloway Standard of the time reported:

"THE LATE SUPERINTENDENT OF THE BURGH POLICE

Mr David Anderson, superintendent of the Dumfries burgh police, died on Wednesday morning (8th June) after a protracted illness. Soon after coming here from Inverness, about a year ago, his health gave way and he grew gradually weaker; and about three months since the disease of which he expired – a pulmonary complaint – began to manifest itself.

The deceased was interred yesterday in St Mary's churchyard, the funeral procession starting from the Council Chambers, to which the body had previously been removed. The hearse was followed by Mr Anderson's four sons, ranged next to them were the whole staff of the burgh police and several constables from the county, the Magistrates and Town Council came next in order, and last of all a numerous body of the inhabitants. The deceased was about '45' years of age."

Chapter Seven
SUPERINTENDENT WILLIAM MITCHELL

The burgh was again looking for a superintendent of police and in early 1859 they advertised the position.

The applicants for the post consisted of:

Benjamin Dickson of Berwick,
William Mitchell of Dumfries,
W. J. Patterson of Kirkcudbright,
William Niven of Kirkcudbright and
Thomas Forsyth of Lanark.

From this short list the commissioner selected William Mitchell.

William Mitchell was born at Dalton, Dumfriesshire in 1827 and was married to Elizabeth Mitchell who was born in 1831 at Kirkcudbright. They had six children, James (born at Urr), Euphemia (born at Langholm), Mary born at Langholm) while William, Elizabeth and John were born at Dumfries. Upon appointment as superintendent of the burgh police the family took up residence in the Midsteeple buildings where they had 4 rooms. Superintendent Mitchell has often been confused with Inspector William Mitchell of the Dumfries County Police who came to the region in 1843 from Dublin Metropolitan Police, although the two are not related.

On 5th March 1860 Colonel Kinloch, HM Inspector of Police implored the Burgh Police commissioners to augment their force with that of the Dumfriesshire County Force. Colonel Kinloch also suggested that more constables might be considered and that the police office in Queensberry Street was an unpleasant place as it was dirty and smelled. At the meeting of the next Police Commission his suggestions were considered:

"DUMFRIES POLICE COMMISSION

On Friday 30st march 1860 the ordinary monthly meeting of the Police Commission was held. Present: Provost Leighton (presiding), Baillie Mundell, Treasurer Sir W Broun, Dean Herries, Messrs. Kennedy, McKelvie, Lennox, Fraser, Turner, McCall, Patterson, Brash, Bell, Pagan and Edgar.

The Clerk, after reading the minutes of the last monthly meeting, and also of the special meeting held on the 5th march to consider Colonel Kinloch's letter on the state of the burgh police force, reported that he had written an answer to Colonel Kinloch in terms of the resolution adopted by the commissioners, and had received the following letter from the colonel in reply:

Logia, Kirriemuir

13th March, 1860"
"To William Martin
Town Clerk

Dear Sir – on my return home on Saturday evening the 10th inst. I received your letter of the 6th.
I only performed my duty in pointing out in my letter to Baillie Gordon that by uniting with the county the inhabitants of Dumfries might have the advantages of a more efficient police and at less expense, than by maintaining a separate police of their own. As the authorities appear to consider it to be of more importance to have the sole appointment of superintendent or chief officer, they can do so by remaining as they are at the present. It will not be easy to find an equal, still less a superior, to the present chief constable of the county in experience or ability as a police officer.
With regard to my opinion of your police office as expressed in my letter to Baillie Gordon, I only repeated what I said in the office itself, and, I thought, loudly and plainly enough to have both been heard and understood by all those who were present.
I think Mr Mitchell, your superintendent, will recollect my remarking very freely and plainly upon what I considered the dirty and slovenly state of the office.
But I do not think Mr Mitchell is at all to blame in the matter: he like other officers in his position, must take and put up with such places and premises as the authorities provide for them and the police business and the men under them.
What I particularly noticed as unusual in the office of a police or any other public establishment was first, the offensive smell of oil and lamps, from these being in the room in which the constables assemble, and the air of which is partly admitted into the prisoners cells; and there appeared to be no ventilation except when the door was open.
Then there was the clothing and accoutrements (great coats and belts) stolen property (generally dirty and filthy articles and particularly what I then saw when I was in your office when I inspected it); and there also appeared to be a quantity of coals in a corner on the floor, but which was so dark as to be difficult to see into.
I do not find all these miscellaneous articles huddled together in the

police offices of other burghs or counties, although some of them are far
from being in perfect order.
That your office is badly situated, and too confined and small for even
the present establishment of police in Dumfries, is a matter in which
I should think there could be but one opinion; but its smallness and
inconvenience appear the more for its being kept well ventilated, sweet
and clean, until a better one can be hereafter provided.
All that can be said is, that it is a little better than the old one. The
cells are small, and appeared to me to require to be more frequently
whitewashed; while one of them had the appearance of being damp. I
beg to assure you that I do not volunteer these remarks or opinions. On
referring to the 65th Section of the Act, you will see that it is my duty:
"to visit and inquire into the state of the police stations, charge rooms,
cells or lockups, and other premises occupied for the use of such police
and to report generally upon such matters, etc". It is my duty: to report
the truth of the state in which I find them; and Baillie Gordon having
expressed a wish that I should write to him a letter containing my
opinion of your police, and what I considered desirable to improve it, I
gladly complied with his request.
I am yours faithfully
JOHN KINLOCK"

The Commission discussed the content of the letter at length and decide to
just drop the matter.

At the same meeting the superintendent's report was read:

"The ordinary monthly report of the superintendent was read by the
Clerk. It stated that during the past month there was a considerable
decrease in crime in the burgh, as compared with the month preceding.
The tabular statements of apprehensions, convictions, fines &c, showed
that 41 males and 10 females had been brought before the magistrates
for various offences during the month. In 30 of these cases the persons
were convicted, 11 were acquitted, 7 remitted to the Sheriff, and in three
cases the proceedings were abandoned. The fines imposed were in all,
£4: 16 shillings of which £4:9 shillings and 6 pence was recovered. The
value of stolen property reported to the police was £15; 17 shillings and
6 pence of which £13: 16 shillings was recovered. The report stated
further that the fire-engine and house were in good conditions, but
reminded the commissioners that a proper reel for the conveyance of the
new hose had not yet been procured."

In addition to the usual monthly report, the following special report by
Superintendent Mitchell was also read:

"As directed at your special meeting on 5th inst., to report my opinion
"upon the police Force, its numbers and efficiency", I beg leave to state

that, as yet, I have always found the present numbers of the force to be most assiduous and attentive to their duties: and as far as number go, I consider that they perform their duties in as satisfactory a manner as any other force.

However, when we take into consideration the lengths of the beats that the eight constables have to patrol, and the small number of men on duty during the day, it will at once been seen that the same amount of protection cannot be given as would be afforded if the force was more numerous, and the beats less extent.

In my report for the month of August last, I suggested that an additional constable should be appointed, and I still think that considerable advantage would be derived from adopting that course. The following quotation from the aforesaid report will show the proposed arrangement: "If an additional constable is appointed the arrangement would be as follows: namely – Two men on duty from 6 a.m. till 9 p.m.; one man on duty from 9 a.m. till 12 p.m.; and four men on duty from 9 p.m. till 6 a.m. The men on night duty would not then be required on day duty except of Wednesdays, but they would come on duty two hours earlier on the Saturday evenings. There would also be additional advantage of another man from 9 p.m. till 12 p.m., at which hour the streets would generally be quiet.

The second plan proposed by the Government Inspector (Colonel Kinloch) in his letter to Baillie Gordon, which was read at the last meeting – namely, "increase the force to ten men" – would provide for a regular system of patrol being carried out during both day and night. I, of course, would wish to see that plan adopted, as it would greatly increase the security of property, &c: but at the same time I consider that the magistrates and Commissioners are the best qualified parties to form a correct judgement of the efficiency or inefficiency of the force, and of the number of constables requisite for the proper performance of the duty, and I would not therefore under present circumstances recommend you to incur so much additional expense.

One of the vents in the police office is in a very bad state of repair, and I have to request that you give orders to have the necessary repairs on it executed.

I enclose a letter received by me from the Government inspector since your last meeting, explaining some statements in his letter to Baillie Gordon as to the state of the office when inspected by him, and which I will thanks you to cause to be read:

The letter to Superintendent Mitchell from Colonel Kinloch is as follows:

Logie, Kirriemuir

13th March 1860"
"To Superintendent Mitchell

Dear Sir – On my return home I have received a letter from Mr Martin,
the Town Clerk of Dumfries, in which he appears to consider that I
have blamed you in a letter I wrote to Baillie Gordon, for the dirty and
slovenly state of the police office at Dumfries on the occasion of my
recent inspection. I beg to reassure you that I do not consider that you
are to blame in the matter.
If you and your men are obliged to keep lamps, and oil and dirty articles
of stolen property, and coals, and clothing all together in a small, low
roofed, and ill ventilated room, it appear to me to be impossible for you
or any other man to keep it sweet, clean, or in the manner that a public
office ought to be kept. If you were provided with suitable premises for
the duties you have to perform in such a large and important town as
Dumfries, I feel confident that you would keep them in a proper and
creditable manner. – I am your faithfully
JOHN KINLOCK"

After discussion by the Police Commission the matter of the extra constables
was set aside until funding for the extra constable could be assessed.

On 10th June 1961 HM Inspector of Police, Colonel Kinloch reported all the
local polices forces. The entry against Dumfries is brief but interesting:

"Burgh of Dumfries – Population in 1861, 10440, strength of force, 10,
Population to each constable, 1044. One superintendent, one sergeant,
and eight constables in three classes. There were three resignations and
two dismissals in the force during the year. The office and cells are now
in good order, and the force is efficient."

During December that year Thomas Fraser, John Christie, William Campbell,
James Lockerbie and Andrew Dempster were appointed constables.

On 16th November 1861 the police commission met:

"The superintendent's report was then read as follows: In laying this
report before you, I have to state that during the six weeks that have
elapsed since you last meeting, the burgh, generally speaking, has been
in a quiet state. That with the exception of one very aggravated case of
assault, nothing of a criminal nature requiring your special attention
has occurred. The total number of persons apprehended is 164, being
an increase of 37 over the number apprehended during the corresponding
period last year. Of the number apprehended, 151 have been convicted,
10 acquitted, 2 remitted to the sheriff, and against one, no proceedings
have been taken.

The usual tabular statements were also read, and the following part of
the superintendent's report to which the Provost called attention: -On
the 19th inst. I reported to the meeting of the bench Constables Robert

Smith and Thomas Wilson, and supernumerary constables William Smith and Alex Cowper, for neglecting their duty on the morning of Wednesday the 6th and Thursday the 7th inst., in the manner more particularly mentioned in the defaulters book herewith produced. This complaint Constables Wilson and Smith endeavoured to repel by making another complaint against me, whereupon the magistrates present agreed to recommend to you at your first meeting to appoint a committee to investigate the different charges. As I am anxious that a thorough investigation should at once be made, I have to request that if the recommendation of the magistrates be adopted, the inquiry should take place with a little delay as possible.

-The Provost moved that the report be adopted, and thought it would be injudicious to enter into consideration of the later part of it. The magistrates had not the power, in his opinion, to suspend any of the men. He was anxious that a committee should be appointed immediately to inquire into the charges of the superintendent against the men, and their charges against him. Several gentlemen having spoken to the same effect, the bench, with Messrs. Ewing, Smith, Patterson and Turner, were appointed as a committee of inquiry, with full power to dismiss any defaulters and the committee would meet that night."

The commissioners examined all the allegations against the superintendent and the constables. The superintendent was found not guilty and that the charges libelled against him were frivolous, but Constables Robert Smith, Alexander Cowper and Thomas Wilson were found guilty and dismissed. Constable William Smith was reprimanded, but was later arrested on a charge of theft.

The General and Police Improvement (Scotland) Act, 1862 (25 & 26 Vict. c.101) was introduced. This set out again the powers of police burghs. It also introduced a system by which commissioners of burghs could apply to the county sheriff for an extension of the burgh boundaries.

On 13th January 1862 Mary Reid or Timney, a mother of four children, murdered Ann Hannah at Carsfad, Dalry in the Stewartry of Kirkcudbright. On the 8th of April, 1862, she stood charged with the murder of Hannah at Dumfries Circuit Court. Upon conviction and having been sentenced to death she cried out "Oh ma weans! My Lord dinna dae that ! I'll no go out. Oh ma weans, oh ma weans! Dinna dae that!"

On the day in question to ensure that the letter of the law was carried out there were 264 police officers on duty; 28 Dumfries County Officers, 7 Dumfries Burgh Officers, 15 Stewartry Officers, 14 Militiamen and 200 Special Constables from the whole region. All constables were ordered to attend in old clothes carrying cutlasses.

The 'Standard' report on 30th April, 1862 is appended in its entirety as it describes the scene in a way that no contemporary writer could hope to emulate:

"EXECUTION OF MARY TIMNEY

The nature and circumstances of the crime for which Mary Reid or Timney suffered the last sentence of the law yesterday morning in Dumfries are so fresh in the memory of our readers that we do not need to do more than refer to them in the briefest terms. The deed for which she was condemned and executed was of a truly horrible description. Her neighbour, Ann Hannah, was found, on the 13th January, lying weltering in her blood on the floor of the little farmhouse at Carsphad, in the district of the Glenkens, under circumstances which though purely circumstantial, pointed out Mary Timney as the perpetrator of the deed. No one was present save the two women when the destructive outrage was committed; and no one is able to describe all that passed as the fatal blows were struck which deprived Ann Hannah of life. She was dreadfully beaten on the head and otherwise wounded; and died unable to name her assailant – breathing twice only 'Oh dear:' before she expired. Strange to say, the person who first discovered the deceased in this condition had been sent for by the convict Timney. To come and bake for her that day; and but for this circumstance the crime probably would not have been discovered until evening, when the brothers of the deceased, who lived with her, came home from their work, and by that time all the salient evidence of the convict's guilt might have been destroyed. This in itself favours the idea that the murder was not premeditated or deliberately intended, but committed in a paroxysm of fury. Mary Timney on being apprehended denied all knowledge of the crime; but her blood dyed garments, and a mallet also stained with blood, found hidden in her house, supplied powerful testimony of her guilt. She was tried at the late circuit court in Dumfries on a charge of having murdered Ann Hannah, was found guilty, and sentenced to death, without hope of mercy, by the presiding judge, Lord Deas.

Strenuous exertions were made with a view to getting the capital sentence commuted; it is superfluous to repeat that these were unavailing. On Friday a letter from the Home Office, addressed to Mrs. McCulloch, Castle Street, apprised the petitioners on behalf of the unfortunate convict that their prayer could not be complied with. A letter to Mr. Ewart, MP, from the same quarter, and the same date (April 24th) also announced that, 'after the most careful consideration of all the facts of the case, and after communication with the judge who presided at the trial, Sir George Grey regrets that he cannot see any ground which would justify him in recommending that the prerogative of the Crown should be interposed for the remission of the capital punishment.' Mr. Ewart, who has done his utmost to promote the views of the petitioner, says in a note dated April 26th which accompanied by the official document. 'It is my melancholy duty – though I cannot doubt that you have received a similar intimation already – to send you the unfavourable answer of the Home Secretary to our intercession for the unhappy convict, Mary Timney. It appears to me that they might have inferred the possibility of a fatal issue, arising (in the beginning) from no premeditated intent to kill. But, alas, the result is otherwise. You and our other friends all enjoy the satisfaction of having used every effort on the tide of Christian mercy. The rest we must submit to Heaven.' As illustrative of Mr. Ewart's untiring zeal in this unhappy business, he made a last appeal in connection with it to the Home Secretary on Monday 29th inst., which he notices in the following terms in a communications of the same date: 'I am afraid that before this letter reaches you, all will be over. As a final attempt, I have just been reviewing the case with Sir George Grey, and bringing again before him the main points on our side. But he has made up his mind. I should have been so glad to telegraph to you an opposite conclusion. But, alas there is no chance.'

The letter from the Home Secretary to Mrs. McCulloch was accompanied by a long private communication to that lady, in which Sir George Grey mentioned in some detail the considerations which induced him to give an unfavourable decision. It is worthy of being stated also, that while the petition from Dumfries praying for a commutation were in course of signature, Mrs. McCulloch under the impression that the petition would be brought directly under the notice of Her Majesty, addressed a letter to the Queen, in which the royal clemency was implored for the prisoner. This letter was forwarded for presentation to Sir William Dunbar, one of the Lords of the Treasury, who duly acknowledged same. Thinking that there was still room to reason the matter, and that there was yet a faint ray of hope, Mrs. McCulloch, in acknowledging the receipt of the Home Secretary's letter, brought again before his mind a variety of considerations, shewing that justice would not be sacrificed to mercy were the convict's sentence commuted to penal servitude. A courteous letter from the Home Secretary, embodying his final answer in the negative, was received on Tuesday morning by Mrs. McCulloch, soon after the unhappy woman for whose life she had pleaded so eloquently and persistently had perished on the scaffold.

All along, the officials of the prison did their utmost to prevent the convict from knowing that any efforts were being made to get her life spared, till it was ascertained that these efforts had proved unavailing. She appears, however, to have imagined that the confession made by her, of having killed Ann Hannah in a quarrel, with no intent to commit murder, might have exercised an influence on her fate, and she having on Saturday hinted to that effect. Mr Cowans, the chaplain, conjured her to relinquish the delusive hope; and when earnestly urged by him to release the sad truth that her hours were numbered, she shook with terror, and seemed overwhelmed with grief. Day by day, her bodily frame became weaker, and it looked at times as if the powers of nature would give way before the executioner arrived to do his hurtful work. Throughout the nights of Saturday and Sabbath last, 'Sleep, that knits up the ravelled sleeve of care,' scarcely ever visited the prisoner's eyelids, so great was the agony she endured, and so shattered was her whole nervous system; and so confused had she become, that she rose unusually early on Monday morning, in the belief that her last hour was at hand. He mental anguish was, there is reason to fear, caused as much, if not more, by the dread of an approaching painful death on the scaffold, as by a sincere heartfelt remorse or a lively contrition on account of her awful crime. The good chaplain, however is not, without hope that she was eventually brought to see in some measure the position she occupied as a guilty bloodstained sinner in the sight of God, and to look for salvation to the atoning sacrifice of Christ. Even in her most penitential moods, she never for once varied from the statement in her confession, as to the circumstances in which the murder was committed; and it will be seen that, in her last words on this subject – her dying declaration, as they may be called – she adhered to the allegation that she had quarrelled with Ann Hannah, but did not intend to take her life.

On Monday evening about 7 o'clock, whilst the chaplain was fervently praying for her spiritual welfare of the prisoner, she fell into a hysterical fit, in which she remained for several hours. Dr. Scott, medical officer of the prison, was at once called in, and remained for a considerable period; and she, under his kindly care having gradually recovered, was put to bed and slept well all the night, two female attendants waiting upon her in the cell. She has been the object of extreme pity and solicitude to all who have had to attend upon her; and to Mr. Stewart, the humane governor of the prison, and Mrs. Stewart, as well as to Mr. Cowans, she has repeatedly expressed her grateful thanks. However it may be accounted for, we simply state a fact which all the prison officials would readily substantiate, that the woman who was depicted on the day of her trial as a savage and implacable monster, without a single redeeming feature in her character or her crime, exhibited during her latter days of her imprisonment, when not visited by the thoughts of her approaching doom, a subduedness of disposition allied to that of those who in the country districts are called 'innocents,' because they are harmlessly idiotical. On Wednesday, the prisoner, as we have previously stated, was visited by her husband and youngest child save one, and by her mother and sister. Her husband had a parting interview with her on Monday; and her farewell words to him were to. 'Remember the weans,' and see that they were brought up well.

The same day, she dictated a letter to her mother and her sister and also one to Mrs. and Miss McCulloch. The composition of the last named letter is that of the female attendant, but the sentiments expressed were the prisoners own; and they are ratified by her signature, Mary Timney, which is tolerably well written for a woman of her rank in life. After thanking the ladies for their, 'Very great kindness,' in striving to get her life 'spared a little longer,' to her poor dear children, she adds, ' I did not intend to kill Ann Hannah – this is the truth I speak. I feel comfort in trusting my soul to Jesus Christ, my only saviour. Oh that he may give me strength to part from this world of sorrow!' A postscript is subjoined, in which she returns sincere thanks to the public of Dumfries for the great interest they have taken on her behalf. The prisoner, after having these statements put upon paper for her expressed a 'desire' to copy the letter in her own handwriting, but the task was too great for her, and before she had made much progress she swooned away. The melancholy fragment lies before us. It is scrawled in these terms, 'Dumfries Prison, 28th April, 1862. – To Mrs. And Miss McCulloch, Castle Street. Dear Ladies. I feel more thankful than I am able to say for the very great kindness you have shewn me in striving to get my life spared a little.' The miserable wretch could go no further – she broke down and fainted when the next words met her eye, 'To my poor dear children.' Truly this tragedy of Carsphad has been a dreadful business from beginning to end: the chief actor in it has died many deaths, and the most sanguinary had 'supped full horrors' enough from it, without being surfeited and causing the general public to be shocked with the scene of yesterday between the odious finisher of the law and his maniacal victim.

On Monday evening all the preparations for the protection of the peace and safety of the community during the carrying into execution the dread sentence of the law were completed. Barriers were erected in the approaches to the prison. At the east end of Buccleuch Street, a strong barrier seven feet high made of flooring laid edgeways between two stout joists fixed deeply into the ground, was carried from the English Chapel to the house opposite. In the centre of it there was a T gate, so that any crush or surge of the crowd in Castle Street could have no effect upon those in Buccleuch Street. From Mr. Mckay's Ironmongery Warehouse, another barrier stretched across the street, while another protected the new U.P. Church buildings from intrusion. Where St. David Street joins Friars Vennel, and fully half road between Friars Vennel and Buccleuch Street, in St. David Street, barriers were erected; and two were also in situation, at some distance apart, to the south of the prison door in Buccleuch Street. The railings of the areas in Buccleuch Street were also protected from being crushed in by stout props between the top bars and the houses opposite which they were erected. Groups lingered about the east corner of the jail-yard all day – moving here and there as if trying to find out where would be the best places to get a good view continually

moving out and in the barriers. In fact, the town had a busy aspect,
and strangers, but for the serious aspect of the people, might have
thought it was the eve of some joyous holiday, instead of that of a day
of doom. There was a continual stir until midnight, when the barriers
were cleared by the police.

Yesterday morning dawned thick and heavy, a dense mist resting on
the houses in town, and shrouding the landscape as with a winding
sheet. It seemed as if nature had put on a veil to screen her from the
horrid spectacle. As early as four o'clock the crowd had commenced to
gather in Buccleuch Street, and the stream of human beings continued
to set in there without intermission till the execution was over. By far
the greatest number of those present were young lads, and labouring
men, apparently from the country. There was also a good many
women present. To the credit of any townsfolk be it spoken, the crowd
was small, and it has been calculated that there were not more than
from two to three thousand persons present. They behaved with great
decorum, and there was none of that jesting at death by shouting,
catcalling, hustling each other, which is said to characterise the
behaviour of such mobs in metropolitan cities. The greatest disturbance
of the peace seemed to us to be an itinerant preacher, who with good
intentions, no doubt, had established himself among the crowd opposite
the U.P. Church, and during the whole morning - from seven o'clock
till nine, with one short interval – continued to harangue the masses
around him in a dissonant tone of voice, which fell harshly on the
ear amid the comparative stillness. All the entrances were guarded
by policemen, and no crushing or tumult occurred. The arrangements
for the accommodation and control of the crowd were very complete,
and were highly creditable to our civic authorities, who have had no
experience in providing for such an assemblage at that which was in the
town on Tuesday morning.

About seven o'clock the Provost and Magistrates, preceded by their
halberdiers, entered within the barriers in Buccleuch Street from the
south, and proceeded at once to the Court-house, where the special
constables sworn in for the occasion had assembled. There were two
hundred special constables present, and they quite filled the jurymen's
and other seats on the area.

Provost Gordon, who took his seat on the bench, called upon the Rev.
Mr. Gray of the New Church, who offered up a prayer suitable for the
occasion. The provost expressed his gratification at the large muster of
constables, and regretted that it had been necessary to summon their
assistance on such an occasion. He asked Mr. Martin, Town Clerk, to
call the roll. On this being done it was found that there was not more
than one absent. The Provost again expressed his gratification at the
manner in which the constables had answered his commons, though

he did not expect that they would be called upon to do anything. The barriers, he said, had been put up to prevent accidents from the crowd, and principally to prevent entrance being obtained to the U.P.Church in course of erection in Buccleuch Street. Mr. Jones, the chief constable of the Dumfries-shire constabulary, would take command of them, and Mr. Johnstone, chief constable of the Kirkcudbrightshire police, and Mr. Mitchell, superintendent of the Burgh police, would also be present to render assistance in case of necessity.

Mr. McGowan, draper, objected to the special constables being controlled by Mr. Jones: they should, he thought, be allowed to choose a captain from amongst themselves. (Hear, hear)

The Provost was quite agreeable to their doing so, and Mr. Pike, surgeon – dentist, colour sergeant of the Dumfries Rifle Corps, was unanimously elected captain.

The constables then left the Court-house, and with several of the rural police forces occupied a considerable space opposite the Court-house and end of St. David Street within the inner barriers which had been reserved for them. The staff of the militia, fully accoutred and armed, and accompanied by a bugler, were drawn up inside the railings of the Court-house.

At twenty minutes from eight o'clock the Provost and Magistrates entered the prison, and Mr. Martin having drawn out a formal receipt for the living woman, Mrs. Timney, she was handed over by the prison governor into the custody of the burgh. The proceeding was merely a formal, but is required by the law on the subject. The Provost and Magistrates then came out into the open space in Buccleuch Street, and the Rev. Mr., Gray having taken his stand on the entrance steps of Mr. T.H. McGowan's residence, next door to the Court-house, and where he could be seen and heard by a portion of the crowd, gave out the first four verses of the 51st Psalm.....

The singing of the Psalm was led by Mr. Wright, New Church preceptor, and the plaintive notes of the tune, St. Paul's, rose in mournful and solemnising cadence above the suppressed hum of the crowds outside the barriers. Mr. Gray at the conclusion of the singing engaged in prayer, with great earnestness and fervour supplicating the Most High on behalf of the poor woman whose hours on earth were numbered. Three verses of the 8th Paraphrase were afterwards sung.....

It struck eight o'clock as the last line of the paraphrase was being sung.

The Provost and the Magistrates accompanied by several of the Commissioners of Police, re-entered the prison at quarter past eight, at

which time Calcraft (William Calcraft, the City of London Executioner)
was engaged pinioning the poor woman. The Magistrates and other
gentlemen admitted into the prison proceeded to the court yard of the
building whence a distinct view of the scaffold could be obtained. The
culprit at this time had lost all the composure and fortitude which
she seemed to have obtained from the counsel and consolations of
the chaplain and warders, and shrieked aloud in abject terror. Her
cries, which were most heart rending rung though the empty corridors
and cells, and must have been distinctly heard by the other inmates
of the prison. Even then, when death was staring her in the face, she
declared that she had not murdered Ann Hannah, and that, ' It was
Ann Hannah that struck her first,' She moaned and cried piteously, and
besought them not to hang her, as she was only a young woman.

Calcraft is a squat, sturdy, hard visage, oldish man. A profusion of
curly iron grey hair around his face, gives him a burl expression of
countenance, but he has anything but a jolly look.

He was accompanied by a seedy, swellish sort of barefaced fellow, who
ranks as his assistant, but who, it is said, is a gentleman of independent
means, and has taken to the business from a liking he has for it! Gossip
also has it, that he was the executioner of Palmer, the notorious Rugeley
poisoner. Both men appeared beyond the power of excitement.

The gibbet, which is a hideous erection, had been put up overnight,
and reared its black timbers on the vacant space between the end of
the jail and St. David Street, with the suspending beam pointing to the
north. At twenty minutes past eight o'clock, the culprit was brought out
under the superintendence of Mr. Stewart, governor of the prison, and
accompanied by Mr. Cowans, the chaplain, whose kind ministrations
followed her even to the drop. On being brought out, the prisoner seemed
in a most frantic and distracted state. The crushing agony of the last
three weeks seemed to have had a great effect on both mind and body.
Her countenance had lost all the firmness, stolidity, or stupidity which
it wore during the trial; fear of some great and incomprehensible danger
was impressed on every lineament, and she seemed to have grown
twenty years older since the day of her trial. When she reached the
open air, she gazed round her, and looked up to the blue sky and the
objects around with a kind of idiotic, maniacal, or hysteric stare. It was
remarked in our hearing that she had become insane, and had it not
been for the words she uttered in her great distress, it would have been
difficult to convince us that the 'lamp of reason' had not wavered and
gone out. She screamed aloud, in tones that brought a shudder to the
hearts of those who heard her, 'Oh no, no! Oh no!' 'Oh: my four weans!
Oh: my four weans,'

William Calcraft, Public Executioner

She was just beyond the prison wall on to the platform when a packet, in apparent great haste, was delivered to the governor of the prison. The eyes of those that witnessed its delivery were riveted upon Mr. Stewart, and recollections of reprieves to prisoners when on the scaffold flashed like electricity through the minds of every one. With a disdainful toss the papers were cast aside, and it appears it was merely a request from some impudently enterprising news-agent in London for particulars of the execution in time for the evening papers.

While the convict was being brought forward to the steps leading to the drop, she caught sight of the gentlemen in the court yard of the prison, and looked towards them with an imploring look, crying out, 'Oh my four weans!' Uttering this cry in accents which were piteous and heart rending in the extreme, she was assisted on to the drop. On her appearing there, the state of excited suspense in which the crowd had been held was broken by wailing ejaculations of pity and commiseration, which rose like a great sigh in the quiet morning air. She continued in plaintive beseeching accents to cry, 'Oh no!' 'Oh my four weans!' and asked to get standing a little, while the hangman was busy about his preparations. She was supported while Calcraft, with considerable dexterity, and a great coolness and deliberation, took of her mutch or cap, drew the white cap over her face, adjusted the noose upon her neck, fastened the rope to the cross beam, and at twenty three minutes past eight o'clock, drew the bolt. The unfortunate woman dropped about fifteen inches. Death to all appearance was painless and easy, and the execution, who must be allowed to be a good judge in such matters, said she died instantly. She only gave one desperate convulsive struggle after the drop fell, the twitching of the fingers apparent for some time after life was extinct were supposed to arise solely from nervous or muscular action.

When the bolt was drawn, a thrill of horror chilled every heart. One of the gentlemen in the prison yard almost fainted, and two of the militiamen drawn up opposite the Court-house, literally fell out of the ranks. From the crowds outside arose a cry of distress as if the ground had been opening to swallow them up.

The body, a hideous spectacle in the calm, blue, sunny April morning hung fully thirty minutes – the customary time – exposed to the gaze of the vulgar crowds on the streets, from whom solitary cries of pain and distress arose at intervals. As the body hung on the gibbet, the mist lifted, and the sun shone out brightly. At five minutes from nine o'clock, the corpse was lowered into the arms of officers in waiting, and carried into the prison.

The crowds quietly dispersed, the special constables give up their batons, and at ten o'clock the town had regained its ordinarily quiet aspect; but

Depiction of the execution carried in the Dumfries and Galloway Standard at the time.

the unspeakable horror of that awful morning scene will long haunt and harass the minds of the onlookers."

On 30th January 1863 Thomas Fraser and Robert Little were appointed as constables, while John Moor was suspended and eventually reprimanded regarding his intemperate habits. He was dismissed in October that year having been found drunk yet again.

On 9th April 1863 the below was issued by Chief Constable John Jones of the Dumfriesshire County police:

In May 1864 James Cavet and John McColl were appointed and the superintendent was awarded £60 per year as superintendent and a further £30 per year as Inspector of Cleansing. The number of constables was fixed at six plus the sergeant and the commissioners agreed to provide a night sergeant to supervise the constables between 9pm and 4am.

On 30th September 1864 John Turner Scott was appointed constable and immediately made the night sergeant. On 10th October he resigned the position.

At this time Superintendent Mitchell was convicted at the Sheriff Court of assault and sentenced to two months imprisonment. There was a popular outcry for the post to remain open for him, but he saved the police commissioners the trouble by resigning. Initially the resignation was not accepted and they held out in the hope that they could reinstate him, but the Government intervened and the stalemate was only resolved when Superintendent Mitchell resigned again.

Never one to be beaten Mr. Mitchell then turns up again in 1867 when he applied for, but was refused, a grocers permit from the commissioners of police for a shop at 26 St Michael's Street. He turns up again in 1868 as a constable in Maxwelltown Municipal Police. He was later promoted to Maxwelltown Burgh Sanitary Inspector, a significant position in those days.

On 31st January 1866 the following advertisement was published:

"WANTED FOR DUMFRIES BURGH POLICE

A SUPERINTENDENT to undertake the Charge of this Force and perform the other Duties required of him under the Police Act. Salary: £100 per annum. He will require to enter upon his duties upon 1st March next.
Applications, stating age, and with Certificates of Character and Qualifications, must be lodged with me on or before 21st February next.

W.M. Martin, Clerk of Police
Dumfries, 29th January 1866"

Chapter Eight
SUPERINTENDENT/CHIEF CONSTABLE JOHN MALCOLM

On 23rd February 1866 a short list of suitable candidates for the new Dumfries Burgh Superintendent was drawn up:

1) Alexander Croll, Portobello,
2) John Malcolm, Kirriemuir,
3) Daniel McDonald, Dumbarton,
4) William Morrison, Leith,
5) James Gordon, Tain and
6) John Anderson, Bathgate.

After interview the short list was reduced to Alexander Croll and John Malcolm. Malcolm won the vote and in March 1866, John Malcolm, aged 39 years, was appointed as the Superintendent of Dumfries Burgh Police. Mr. Malcolm came from Kirriemuir, Fife, where he had been Superintendent and Procurator Fiscal. Mr. Malcolm, who was born in 1831, was the son of Michael Malcolm a linen weaver and his wife Helen; He died at his home at 3 Whitesands, Dumfries in 1903 of heart disease and cerebral apoplexy aged 72 years.

Upon taking up his post Mr. Malcolm noted that there were ten officers in the Dumfries Burgh Police and, within the Royal Burgh of Dumfries, there were 117 ale and liquor licences in force, a situation he was to address vigorously over the next few years.

In 1867 a new Town Hall was erected in Buccleuch Street, Dumfries on the site of the former court house: opposite the new sheriff court house and prison. These' Municipal Chambers' also became home to the Dumfries Burgh Police who were given a small station house on the ground floor up a close to the east side of the chambers.

As an addendum to the police office in Queensberry Street, the following appears in the press on 8th May 1867 after the burgh police had moved to Buccleuch Street.:

> "...Jacob Dickson applied for a reversion of decision of Dumfries Magistrates by which he was refused a (liquor) licence for the premises lately used as a police office in Queensberry Street. Mr. Gunn appeared

Superintendent John Malcolm

for the appellant, and stated that when his client purchased the property from the town council he did so on the assurance that he would receive a licence for it. He produced a memorial testifying to the character of the appellant, and set forth the desirableness of having such a house in the locality – the names of the following councilors and ex-councillors being amongst the subscriptions: Messrs Ewing, Dunbar, F. Nicholson, Waugh, J. Edgar, Irving, T.H. McGowan. Mr. Martin said there was nothing against the appellant's character; and Baillie Fraser remarked that standing in the 'Square' he could count a dozen licensed houses, so that there could be no neeed for this one: there are 105 public-houses in the town, and this great number he believed to be one of the reasons why so much Sunday traffic prevails. – Baillie Newbiggin said if there was any inducement held out to the appellant when the property was sold it was by Mr. Dunbar, the auctioneer.

Colonel Munroe moved that the appeal be refused, seconded by Baillie Newbiggin; and Mr Mundell, seconded by Ex- Provost Leighton, that it be granted. On a division, Colonel Munroe's motion was carried by a large majority."

There was still a need to recruit constables and on 15th May 1867 the local press contained a recruitment poster:

"Burgh Police Force Dumfries

Wanted for this Force

ONE or TWO Stout, Active, and intelligent MEN, Between 21 and 35 years of Age, and not under 5 Feet 10 Inches in Height. Wages, with Uniform Clothing, 17 shillings and 18 pence, and 19 shillings per Week. Applications, accompanied with Certificates of Character, to be lodged with John Malcolm, Superintendent of Burgh Police Dumfries Burgh Police Chambers, Dumfries 13th May 1867"

Mr. Malcolm was no sooner in post when he had to return to Forfar:

"ACTION OF DAMAGES AGAINST SUPERINTENDENT MALCOLM

We are requested to publish the following in reference to a charge of assault against Mr. Malcolm, Superintendent of the Dumfries Burgh Police Force. While Superintendent of Police in Kirriemuir, On Thursday, Sheriff Robertson issues an interlocutor in the ordinary court, Forfar, is the case at the instance of Betsy Lindsay, against John Malcolm, ex-Superintendent of Police, Kirriemuir, in which he assolized the defender from the conclusions, and found the pursuer liable in expenses.

The circumstances of the case are fully explained in a note subjoined to his lordship's interlocutor. His lordship says: "This action of damages raised against the late Superintendent of Police in Kirriemuir, by the pursuer, who avers that the defender maliciously, and without probable cause, apprehended, and caused her to be detained in the police cells at Kirriemuir, for three hours. She further avers ill treatment and violence on the part of the defender, whereby she suffered bodily injuries. For these wrongs the pursuer claims a hundred guineas by way of solatium and damages. In the opinion of the Sheriff Substitute, the result of the proof taken in the case is to exonerate the defender from any blame in the matter, and to show that the pursuer has greatly exaggerated the circumstances of the apprehension, and founded her claim upon averments which she has completely failed to substantiate. It appears from the proof that the manufacturers in Kirriemuir have often complained of the purloining of yarns from their establishments, and suspected certain persons of this theft; and that the pursuer was one who was commonly purported to deal in purloined yarns. The defender, as Superintendent of Police, was spoken to about this by the manufacturers, and they had blamed him for not putting a stop to it. They had even pointed out the pursuer on several occasions for carrying stolen yarns between certain suspected houses. The purloiners are in the habit of carrying the yarns in baskets, and such receptacles, and as this is done in small quantities at the time it is difficult to detect the theft.

Here then is a system of petty thieving carried out in Kirriemuir; the Superintendent is informed of it, the pursuer is actually pointed out to him as suspected of the crime; so what is more natural or regular that that he should take steps to expose this illegal traffic. One morning he met the pursuer in the street with a basket and a milk flagon; he asked what she had in these, and on her refusing to tell him, or show him what the basket or flagon contained, and upon her endeavouring to get away, he looked into the basket and flagon and found them both packed full of yarns. On this he took her to the police office. These are the facts as proved: and even supposing, for the sake of argument, that the defender had no right without warrant to search the basket and flagon, and that he did so on his own peril and responsibility – even in this case the result of the search would have amply exonerated him and justified the means taken to detect the crime, for it is proved his suspicions were well grounded. But the Sheriff Substitute holds that the defender, under the circumstances, was justified in searching and apprehending without any warrant at all The fact of the pursuer having been pointed out to the police as suspected, that fact that she endeavoured to conceal the basket she carried and when asked what she had in the milk flagon she refused to tell, and that she tried to get away from the police, all this confirmed the suspicions of the defender, and justified him in apprehending". As for the complaint that the pursuer suffered bodily injuries, "the medical evidence satisfies the Sheriff Substitute that

*she was in no way injured by the police": and in regard to the thisrd
complaint he is of the opinion that "the term of three hours" cannot
be called and unreasonable delay, or excessive detention, nor can it be
called an act of oppression or tyranny on the part of a police officer who
during that time is doing all he can to test the truth of the apprehended
party's statement, and get advise as to the party's liberation. For these
reasons the Sheriff Substitute has assolized the defender."*

About 8am on the morning of May 12th 1868 Scotland's last public hanging
took place at Dumfries Prison in Buccleuch Street Dumfries. The Prisons Bill
had just passed through Parliament and this bill was to stop public executions
forever. A crowd of over 3000 people gathered to witness the sentence passed
on Robert Smith aged 19 years from Eaglesfield.

Robert Smith a 19 year old labourer had been orphaned aged eight and found
work in a limekiln aged thirteen. He was charged and convicted of the Rape,
Murder and Robbery of an eleven year old girl, Thomasina Scott at Croftshead
plantation near Cummertrees on 1st February that year. Having raped and
strangled her with a boot lace; he then stole 9 Shillings and 11 pence from
her (48p) and attempted to murder a witness, Mrs. Crichton who had seen
him with his victim earlier that day. Fortunately for Mrs. Crichton, Smith was
disturbed by a neighbour and fled the scene before she too was murdered.

Smith was traced later that day by Chief Constable Malcolm of the Burgh
Police in a lodging house in Dumfries.

The 'Standard' reported on the charges against Smith as follows:

"THE ANNANDALE MURDER

*.....Robert Smith, prisoner in Dumfries jail: Charged with rape as also
murder, as also theft, as also assault by discharging loaded firearms,
and by cutting and stabbing, as also contravention of 10 George 1V, cap
38, section 2 – in so far as , on Saturday, 1st February, 1808, in or near
a wood or plantation called the Croftsheads plantation, on the farm
of Howes, in the Parish of Annan, and on the north side of the public
road leading between the village of Cummertrees and the burgh of
Annan, the said Robert Smith did wickedly and feloniously attack and
assault the now deceased Thomasina Scott, then a girl of nine years of
age or thereby, daughter of John Scott, shoemaker and grocer, at Rigside
Cottage parish of Cummertrees, and did ravish her; and did then and
there forcibly grasp her and compress her neck and throat; and did with
his hands and by means of a cord or other ligature, which he tied or
drew tightly round her neck, strangle or choke the said Thomasina Scott;
and did otherwise maltreat and abuse her; by all which or part thereof,
the said Thomasina Scott was grievously and mortally injured, and
in consequence thereof, immediately or soon after died, and was thus
murdered by the said Robert Smith:*

Likeas (2) the said Robert Smith having so attacked and assaulted and murdered the said Thomasina Scott, did thereafter, time and place above libeled, wickedly and feloniously steal and theftiously away take from the pocket or person of the said Thomasina Scott, nine shillings and eleven pence sterling or thereby in silver and copper money, the property or in the lawful possession of the said John Scott:

Likeas (3) On Saturday the 1st February, 1868, in or near the dwelling house or premises called Longfords Cottage, situated in the parish of Cummertrees, then and now or lately occupied by Robert Crichton, farm servant or farm, manager, residing there, the said Robert Smith did, wickedly and feloniously, attack and assault Jane Patterson or Crichton, wife of the said Robert Crichton, and did with a pistol loaded with powder and leaden shots or pellets, willfully, maliciously, and unlawfully shoot the said Jane Peterson or Crichton, and the contents of said pistol did strike and wound the said Jane Peterson or Crichton on or about her head; and the said Robert Smith did seize hold of the said Jane Paterson or Crichton, and did with a knife, willfully, maliciously, and unlawfully cut or stab her on or near the neck and throat, with intent to murder or to maim, disfigure or disable the said Jane Paterson or Crichton, or with intent to do her some other grievous bodily harm; and did force the said Jane Paterson or Crichton down upon the floor and did seize hold of and violently compress her throat or neck with his hands, and did willfully, maliciously and unlawfully attempt to suffocate or to strangle the said Jane Paterson or Crichton, with the intent to murder or disable her, or to do her some other grievous bodily harm – and all which the said Robert Smith did with the intent to kill the said Jane Paterson or Crichton and by all which she was cut, wounded, and bruised, to the great effusion of her blood, serious injury of her person and danger of her life."

The Public Hangman, Mr. Askern, didn't make a clean job of the execution and Smith took fifteen minutes to die. During this period a large number of the assembled crown fled the scene. Smith's death mask is retained at Dumfries Museum.

May 1868 also saw Chief Constable Malcolm prosecuting an assault on one of his constables:

"ASSAULTING A CONSTABLE

Thomas Currie, labourer, Maxwelltown, was charged with assaulting Constable Johstone in Castle Street, while conveying a prisoner to the police office, between ten and eleven o'clock on Saturday night. Being asked whether he was guilty or not Currie replied that he had never lifted his foot to a man in his life.

The hanging of Robert Smith at Dumfries prison in Buccleuch Street

Constable Johstone stated that a crowd of people were following him as he was taking a drunk and incapable along the street, and Currie among others was trying to effect a rescue. The prisoner got violent and they both fell on the street. While down and attempting to secure his prisoner, witness was kicked on the side by Currie who also used threatening language.

The prisoner stated: Mr. Malcolm has mistook this man, sir I never lifted my foot to a man or boy in my life sir and on Saturday I was as sober as any man in this room.

Andrew Bryson, a clerk, corroborated the constable's evidence and had not the slightest doubt that the prisoner was the man he saw committing the assault.

Mr. Malcolm asked the prisoner: Have you any questions to put to the witness? The prisoner said, Yes, but it's no use putting questions. (Laughter from the crowd).

Mr. Malcolm asked: Were you not in the crowd? The prisoner replied: I was not I was coming up High Street.

Mr. Malcolm then addressed the court, stating that the siege to which the constable was subjected was so bad that several persons came to the police office to give information

The Magistrate, in pronouncing judgment said though he could have wished more evidence regarding the identity, he had no doubt that the prisoner was the man who committed the assault, and he would have to consider the penalty of this offence. It was one of a very serious nature and he had rendered himself liable to be fined £10 or sent to prison for sixty days. He did not think he could make the punishment less than 20 shillings or ten days, which was accordingly the sentence of the court.

At the same hearing John Hoy, cattle dealer appeared for being drunk and incapable and was fined 5 shillings: and James Watson being found in a similar condition was forfeited 5 shillings of bail."

On7th May 1869 Mr. Malcolm was appointed Sanitary Inspector of Health under the Public Health (Scotland) Act 1867 and in January 1870 he was further appointed as Burgh Procurator Fiscal on the death of the PF, Mr. George McMinn. At this time his salary was raised to £150 per annum as he was appointed as Inspector of Common Lodging Houses and he took over the supervision of the Burgh Cleansing Department.

The Dumfries and Galloway Standard reports in December 1870:

"Frightening the Lieges;

As repeatedly noticed in our columns great dread prevails around the suburbs of Dumfries, especially southwards, originated, as it is said, by evil-disposed persons who, dressed in white sheets, start up suddenly in the presence of women and children. A notice just issued by the Sheriff offers a reward of £10 for the apprehension of any of these miserable tricksters."

In December 1870 Constables John McMinn and William Kelly called on William Kelly, a publican, who sold drink from his home in Bridge Street. Kelly let the constables into his home but refused to let them enter the room that held the liquor. He was reported and appeared at court where he was fined 20 shillings for preventing the constable's entry into licensed premises.

The Burgh Police Court in August 1870 heard the following trial:

"ASSAULT ON THE POLICE
At the Burgh Court on Monday 8th inst. Provost Harkness, presiding, George Wright, a baker, residing in Dumfries, was charged with an assault on the person of Sergeant Lauder of the Burgh Police Force, by striking him with his clenched fists on the head and face, by all which he was cut and wounded, and also with a breach of the peace by otherwise conducting himself in a very outrageous and disorderly manner. He pleaded guilty. Mr. Malcolm, Procurator Fiscal, in moving for sentence, remarked that this was case of serious character, and arose in this way: Sergeant Lauder was passing along High Street on Saturday evening and was called into the shop of Mr. Dunbar, baker, to eject the prisoner, who was there very much the worse of drink. The sergeant asked him good humouredly to leave the shop and return when sober, but instead of doing so, he attacked the sergeant as set forth in the complaint; the result being that the shop was surrounded by a great number of lads and men, two or three of whom commenced throwing stones by which the plate glass window of the shop was broken. On being secured by other officers who came to the sergeant's assistance, the prisoner was conveyed to the police office, followed by a large crowd; some stones were again thrown and hooting, yelling and shouting at the police were freely indulged in. If such conduct as that were allowed to pass unchecked, the police would soon be powerless, and he (Mr. Malcolm) had no hesitation in moving for such a sentence as would deter the prisoner and others from conducting themselves in a similar manner in future. The provost, in passing sentence said that he himself heard the noise on the street while sitting in his own house, and came out to ascertain the cause, and on arriving at the police office, he saw that the officers had been abused, and that some of them were

bleeding. Now this state of matters could not be allowed. The officers must be protected in the execution of their duty; and as a warning to the prisoner, who appeared to be a respectable man, he could not do less than send him to prison for thirty days without alternative of a fine."

In 1871 the Hon. Charles Carnegie, Inspector of Scotch Constabularies reported that Dumfries Burgh consisted of ten officers. This consisted of one superintendent, two sergeants and seven constables. The superintendent was Procurator Fiscal for the Burgh Justice of the Peace Court and Burgh Sanitary Inspector. Mr. Carnege decreed that the force was efficient.

On 22nd October 1871 George McLean was appointed as constable. He was to serve for 34 years and retired in 1905 with a pension.

On 11th May 1872 the following advertisement appeared:

"BURGH POLICE FORCE DUMFRIES

WANTED FOR THIS FORCE

AN OFFICER to act as DAY SERGEANT, Wages and Uniform Clothing, 22 shillings per week. Sobriety indispensible. Applications in Handwriting of Applicant, stating Age, Height and former Experience, with testimonials of Character, to be lodged with JOHN MALCOLM, Superintendent of Burgh Police, on or before the 20th instant.

Also, an active and Intelligent MAN, under 25 Years of age, and not less than 5 feet 9 inches in height, as CONSTABLE. Wages 18 shillings, 19 shillings and 20 shillings per week.

Burgh Police Chambers, Dumfries
4th May 1872."

The commissioners of Police for the Royal Burgh of Dumfries adopted the Act of Parliament 20 and 21 Victoria Chapter 72 entitled:

'An Act to render more effectual the Police in the Counties and Burghs in Scotland',

This Act created national policing rules. Superintendents of police were thereafter to be called chief constables and police forces found to be efficient were to be awarded Government grants to aid their expenditure. Superintendent Malcolm was thereafter appointed as the first Chief Constable of Dumfries.

In 1876 the Inspector of Constabularies reported that Dumfries Burgh Police consisted of
One chief constable
Two sergeants and
Seven constables.

He further stated that they were an efficient police force and the commissioners were awarded £143:14s:11d towards the costs of running the police. The average age of the force was 27 years, four months and the average height of the officers was 6 feet one inch.

In January 1876 James Murray was appointed. Murray a native of Canonbie served for 34 years and retired in 1910.

Chief Constable Malcolm, was also the Procurator Fiscal for the Burgh Court and Burgh Sanitary Inspector, he received no extra payment for these posts. The force was deemed to efficient under the Police Act.

The 'suspension' bridge that connects the Whitesands with the 'Millgreen' was constructed in 1875 and remains an important link between the two sides of the River Nith.

The present Dumfries Prison at 'Jessiefield' in Maxwelltown, was completed in 1882. This new prison had 78 cells and was set to occupy around 80 prisoners, as well as some accommodation for officers. This replaced the former prison buildings in Buccleuch Street next to the Sheriff Court. As a result the land in Buccleuch Street was freed up and the present Procurator Fiscal's Office was constructed as the new Dumfries Post Office. It was also, for some time, an office of the Revenue. Prior to this the post office was in Queens Street.

In December 1877 the Works Committee met and discussed a plan to turn the cell under the Midsteeple into a shop. The matter was indefinitely delayed as the committee recognized that whole Midsteeple required refurbishment and would cost in excess of £1000 to repair.

On 21st July 1878 Andrew Gibson was appointed; a native of Kincardine, he was 29 years of age when he joined and retired in 1886 as Sergeant.

In September that year William Currie a 30 year old from Irongray joined. He was to serve until 1909 when he resigned. William Stewart, an Aberdonian, joined in June 1881 and resigned in 1888.

On 14th January 1880 the council held their regular meeting:

"SUPERINTENDENTS REPORT

The Clerk read the report of Mr. Malcolm, Superintendent of Police, for the three months ended 31st December, of which the following is an abstract:

Number of persons apprehended during the quarter: 225
(180 males and 45 females)
Convicted: 199
Acquitted: 18
Remitted (To the High Court) 8
Amount of fines imposed: £53: 7 shillings
Of which £47: 10 shillings recovered
Theft reported to the police: 37
Value of stolen property: £40: 9 shillings and 9 pence
Value of property recovered: £30: 10 shillings and 7 pence

The following remarks were appended to the report: The above table of apprehensions shews a decrease of 48 compared with the previous quarter, and an increase of 21 when compared with the corresponding quarter last year. The fines imposed during the previous quarter amounted to £85: 15 shillings, of which sum £53: 8shillings and 6 pence was recovered, while the sum imposed this quarter amounted to £53: 7 shillings, and that recovered to £47: 10 shillings, thus shewing a decrease for the present quarter of £31: 18 shillings on the amount imposed, and a decrease of £5: 18 shillings and 6 pence on the amount recovered. The watching department is in good working order and the present strength of the force is nine. During the past year the number of shops and premises found insecure by the police during the night was 219, intimation of which was given to the occupiers. The Fire Engine and hose are in good condition. Only one fire occurred during the quarter, which was speedily extinguished, and the circumstances reported to the Procurator Fiscal for the county."

In January 1881 the press reported:

"SAD CASE OF HOUSEBREAKING

About 1 o'clock on the Sabbath morning as Constables Webb and Halliday of the Dumfries burgh Police were patrolling High Street and according to custom trying the doors of all business premises, to see that they were securely fastened, they found that the bolt had been drawn *back from the door of the passage which leads to the back premises of Messrs Grierson Brothers, ironmongers on the Plainstanes. On pushing it open the found a young lad who was preparing to make his way out. This turned out to be Henry William Hetherington, aged 18 years, an apprentice in the employment of the firm. On being searched a number of silver plated articles were found upon him; and agreeably to a statement made by himself for on being detected he at once made a full confession. The police found that on the floor of the front shop a bag in which were packed a further quantity of electro-plated goods, also intended to be carried off.*

The lad states that at seven o'clock when he was understood to have gone home, he concealed himself in the water closet at the back yard, where he waited for two hours, until Mr. Grierson had locked up the premises and left for the night. He then emerged from his hiding place and entered the shop by the office window, breaking a pane of glass and undoing the snib. It would thus appear to have been a most bold and determined attempt at robbery, the lad having laid in wait for two hours before he was able to commence operations and having afterwards spent four hours in ransacking the shop and packing his booty; and it is rendered doubly sad by the circumstances of his youth and respectable connections. The total value of articles appropriated is stated to be £16. The following is a list of them: Cream jug, sugar basin, tea kettle, two dish covers, paid nippers, thirteen tea spooks, three whisky flasks, one lady's workbox, sardine box – these all being silver plated, two files, two keys, a screw driver, and five pence in coppers. The accused was brought before Provost Shortridge in the police court on Monday, and remitted to the PF of the Sheriff Court."

In November 1881 John Dickson, 21, from Tinwald, was appointed and retired as a constable in 1815. Samuel Drysdale a 25 year old from Mochrum was appointed in February 1882 only to resign in 1885.

This was swiftly followed by John Dickson from Applegirth who was appointed in 1882 and resigned in 1884. Frederick Crosbie from Kirkmahoe was appointed in March 1883 and resigned in July 1885.

In December 1884 David Hastings a native of Kirkmahoe joined the burgh police and retired as a constable in April 1916.

March 1885 saw John Bonnar from Kinggussie join the force only to be forced to resign in November 1885 due to being drunk on duty, while John Bailey from Kirkcolm, who joined in July 1885, lasted only four years and resigned in 1889. Another short lived recruit, David Murdoch from Sorn joined in September 1885 and resigned in May 1886.

In November 1885 Adam Dunsmore from Fourtowns, County Down, joined the force only to be forced to resign for drunkenness in November 1889.

Robert Fleming a 21 year old from Stoneykirk had a short but interesting career. He joined in July 1886, but was dismissed in February 1888 having been found by his sergeant stripped to the waist engaged in a wrestling match with a fellow Wigtownshire man in a garden some distance from his beat.

William Adams from Aberdeen also joined in 1888, but had to retire due to ill health in 1889. He died shortly afterwards and his widow was offered a small pension.

In February 1888 Robert Stoba a 21 year old from Caerlaverock was appointed, but resigned in 1900 and became a burgh officer. John Brown from Fife joined in 1888 but was dismissed in 1900 from persistent drunkenness.

In February 1889 another Stoneykirk native, James Fleming joined the force only to be dismissed in March 1990 for misconduct at the Swan Hotel. The misconduct is not further defined.

George Jackson from Gretna was appointed in March 1889 only to resign in January 1891.

In December 1889 Christopher Irving was appointed. A native of Kirkpatrick Fleming he was dismissed in December 1893 for co-habiting with the wife of Constable James Martin of Maxwelltown Police. Constable Martin had lodged a complaint with the police commissioners and having upheld the complaint Constable Irving was dismissed as unfit for the office.

Hugh McLean, another Stoneykirk man, was appointed in 1890 but resigned in 1891. The same year James Campbell from Perth was appointed. He was promoted to sergeant in 1899 and then inspector in 1903. He retired in 1922 with thirty one years service. In 1891 William Hunter from Beith joined, but resigned in 1894.

Mr. Malcolm was a remarkable man, he held the offices of Chief Constable, Burgh Surveyor, Fire-master, Procurator Fiscal and he also held the office of Sanitary Inspector. In 1887 acting as Sanitary Inspector he compiled a report on the 'closes' or lanes that made up Dumfries. He reported that:

"There were 102 closes in Dumfries and the report focused on the overcrowded and unsanitary living conditions of more than one-fourth of the town's inhabitants."

The Burgh Police (Scotland) Act, 1892 (55 & 56 Vict. c.55), which came into effect on 15 May 1893, superseded all earlier general and police acts in burghs. Each burgh was now united as a single body corporate for police and municipal purposes. In some cases a previous royal burgh or burgh of barony or regality had continued to exist alongside the police burgh. Any remaining burghs of barony or regality that had not adopted the police acts were implicitly dissolved. Populous places that could become a burgh were now to have a population of 2,000 or more, though where a place with a lower population resolved to adopt the act, it was at the county sheriff's discretion to allow or refuse such an application. Police commissioners were now to be retitled as councillors, headed by a magistrate under whatever title was customary in the burgh.

"CONSTABLE ASSAULTED WITH A GUN

On 20th December 1893 Dumfries Burgh Court before Baillie Kirk, Thomas Brown a labourer, was charged that the preceding Monday he had assaulted Constable Thomas Sturrock of the Dumfries County Police and struck him on the head with a gun and did present it at his head and body and threaten to blow out his brains. Brown, who claimed he was very drunk at the time plead not guilty saying that he didn't know what he was doing.

Constable Sturrock had been standing on the Whitesands near the Caul watching the fish leaping when Brown appeared and attacked him, striking him on the head with the gun and then threatening him as aforesaid. The Constable had not spoken with or even seen Brown approaching.

Taking into account the seriousness of the offence libeled, the Baillie fined Brown one Guinea (£1:10p) with the alternative of thirty days imprisonment."

In December 1893 John Killop from Perth was appointed. He was promoted to sergeant in 1910. In 1894 John Kerr a native of Kirkmichael was appointed and in 1905 he was promoted to sergeant. He retired in 1920.

4th July 1896 saw the following in the press:

"A NOISY AND REACTIONARY BEGGAR

At the burgh police court yesterday morning, before Provost Glover, Archibald Hastings, a vagrant, was charged with being found begging in High Street on the previous day and also with committing a breach of the peace and challenging people to fight and with tripping up Constable Dickson when conveying him to prison. He pled guilty, stating that he was the worse for drink and did not know what he was doing. The PF stated that the accused begged from some young men, and when they said they had nothing to give him he took off his coat and insisted on fighting them. He was one of a class too numerous in the district who made up their minds to do nothing and went about begging. Provost Glover sent him to prison for thirty days."

In August 1896 at Dumfries Sheriff Court, Sheriff Campion passed a sentence of thirty days imprisonment on William Graham a Bacon Curer from Annan. Graham was found guilty of creating a disturbance in Annan show-yard and assaulting Superintendent Peel, and Inspector McIntosh of the Dumfries County Police. At the same hearing the sheriff sent John Coupland, Carter of Noblehill, Dumfries to jail for ten days for assaulting his wife in their home.

"MEETING OF THE WATCHING COMMITTEE

26th November 1898: On Thursday last the Watching Committee of Dumfries Burgh Commission had a meeting with Sergeant Thomson, Perth City Police, and Sergeant Rennie, Kirriemuir, with a view to the appointment of an inspector of police as recommended by Captain Munroe on the occasion of his last inspection. When the two men had withdrawn, Mr. Dykes proposed the appointment of Sergeant Rennie, and Mr. Brunton seconded. Mr. Livingston proposed the appointment of Sergeant Thomson and this was seconded by Mr. Peter Scott. Five voted for the appointment of the Kirriemuir man and four for the Perth sergeant. The appointment rests with the Chief Constable Mr. Malcolm, but he decided to carry the committee along with him on this matter and Sergeant Rennie will accordingly be appointed."

There was, however, a change of plan as the Home Secretary objected to the council's choice and they were asked to consider Sergeant George Stephen Lipp the sergeant at Linlithgow as the new inspector. After consideration George Stephen Lipp was appointed.

"On 10th October 1898 Peter Flynn a labourer appeared at the Burgh Police Court charged with committing a Breach of the Peace in Friars Vennel the previous day and also assaulting one of the police constables by kicking him on the right leg. He admitted the Breach of the Peace, but denied the assault. The police evidence was led to the effect that when the accused was taken into the passage in the police office in front of the cells he lay down and on being lifted up he kicked Constable Killop as stated, knocking him off his feet. Baillie Dinwiddie found the charge proven and sent the accused to prison for seven days without the option of a fine."

In September 1899 Robert Beattie aged 21 from Troqueer was appointed, he retired in 1920.

On 29th May 1901 the burgh inspector George Lipp was in court prosecuting a case of 'furious and reckless driving'.

"THE GLENCAPLE WAGGONETTES

In Dumfries Police Court, Provost Glover on the bench, Robert Cowan,

Chief Constable John Malcolm and the Dumfries Burgh Police Circa 1900
Rear, left to right: unknown; unknown; unknown; Constable R Beattie
Front, left to right: Unknown; Sgt J Campbell: Insp. G.S. Lipp: CC Malcolm: Sgt J Kerr: unknown: Unknown

*'bus driver', Glencaple pleaded guilty to a charge of driving a horse
and waggonette in Irish Street and St Michael's Street on 20th inst.
in a furious and reckless manner. He stated that he had no whip,
but lost control of the brake. Inspector Lipp, who prosecuted, stated
that the accused was dismissed last year for a similar offence. It was
a very dangerous practice. The Provost said, "The magistrates were
fully determined to put the practice down" and he imposed a fine of 7
shillings and 6 pence with the option of five days in jail."*

Mr. Malcolm served as Superintendent and Chief Constable of Dumfries Burgh
Police for 37 years and died in office, aged 72 years, on 16th January 1903, a
short time after he advised the Police commissioners that he intended to take
retirement owing to infirmity through poor health. He had completed fifty
years police service.

On 7th January 1903 Mr. Malcolm's resignation was reported in the press:

"RESIGNATION OF CHIEF CONSTABLE MALCOLM

*We regret to learn that Mr. John Malcolm, who had been laid aside
by illness for some time, finds it necessary on account of the state of
his health to resign the appointments of chief constable and burgh
prosecutor, and that a letter to that effect will be laid before the Town
Council tomorrow. Mr. Malcolm, who is 72 years of age, has served
for fifty years in the police force. His first appointments were in his
native county of Fife. He afterwards for a period of seven years acted
as superintendent of police and procurator fiscal in Kirriemuir, and in
March 1866, he was appointed to the same position in Dumfries, which
he has thus filled for almost 37 years, doing faithfully and discreetly his
duty to the community. His health, we are glad to know, is improving
although he finds rest necessary."*

Chapter Nine
CHIEF CONSTABLE GEORGE STEPHEN LIPP

Chief Constable George Stephen Lipp

George Stephen Lipp, a bachelor, was born on 18th May 1870 at Fordyce, Banffshire. He was the son of Alexander Lipp a farm overseer and his wife, Ann Lipp. He had transferred from Linlithgow, where he was a sergeant with nine years service; to Dumfries Burgh upon appointment as inspector and died a mere six years later 17th January 1909, from tuberculosis whilst still in office as chief constable. His brother, John Lipp from Edinburgh registered the death.

He was promoted to Chief Constable in 1903 to replace Mr. Malcolm who had also died in post.

When Mr. Lipp was promoted to Chief Constable, his post as Inspector of Burgh Police was done away with and the commissioners appointed two constables in his place. These were Donald Gunn aged 22 from Kilmartin and Robert Martin Broadfoot aged 20 from Maxwelltown.

Constables Currie, Murray, unknown and a
Mr. Glendinning at the fountain in High Street in 1903.

The Town Councils (Scotland) Act, 1900 (63 & 64 Vict. c.49) retitled the governing body of a burgh as "the provost, magistrates, and councillors" of the burgh. In certain burghs the title Lord Provost was to be continued.

The Burgh Police (Scotland) Act, 1903 (3 Edw. VII. c.33) amended the 1892 Act and included a number of provisions relating to building within a burgh. The burgh was to maintain a register of plans and petitions (in modern terms a register of planning permissions). Permitted developments were to be issued building warrants by the town council, and the burgh surveyor was empowered to enforce the warrants and rectify unauthorised building. New powers were given to town councils in relation to maintenance of footpaths and public rubbish bins, and the placing of advertisement hoardings and scaffolding. Minimum standards were set for the height and internal space of new buildings and on overcrowding, and for the width of streets. Powers were given to the burgh to make new streets and openings. Also included in the Act were various sundry powers and duties including: the compulsory lighting of vehicles, licensing for billiard halls and ice cream shops, prohibition on betting in the street, powers on controlling milk supply, and penalties for littering.

In September 1904 Angus McPherson from Kilmartin, was appointed. He resigned in 1908 when he joined the Glasgow City Police. James Thomson aged 24 from Johnstone, Dumfries, was appointed and transferred to the Dumfriesshire County Police in 1911.

On 13th December 1905 the 'Standard reports:

"POLICE PROMOTION

Constable John Kerr, of the burgh police, who has been stationed at Noblehill since the extension of the burgh boundaries, has been promoted sergeant in room of Sergeant McLean, who retired from the force on Saturday. Sergeant Kerr, who is an experienced young officer of high character and personal popularity, will assume the duties of his new rank in the beginning of the year."

1905 Constable Thomas Byers Campbell

Constable Number 5, Thomas Byers Campbell served with the Dumfries Burgh Police between 15th June, 1905 and 19th January 1911 before transferring to the Dumfries County Police where he served at Canonbie, Annan and Dalswinton until his retirement in 1934.

On 31st December 1905 the population of Dumfries Burgh was 16,173. The Dumfries Burgh Police consisted of:

Chief Constable George S. Lipp,
Inspector John. Campbell,
Sergeant John Kerr and
Eleven Constables.

The average age of the officers was 35 years, the average height was 5 feet eleven inches and average service was 13 years. The annual cost of the force was £1,411: 9 shillings: 5 pence. A new beat surrounding the area of Noblehill had been added to the list of duty points. Constable Kerr had been promoted to Sergeant replacing Sergeant McLean who retired on pension having completed 34 years service.

Domestic violence is not a new phenomenon and the courts recognised the seriousness and dealt with them accordingly:

"SMART SENTENCE FOR WIFE ASSAULT

15th March 1905:

In Dumfries Police Court on Monday, before Baillie Lennox, Edward Jardine, quarryman, pleaded guilty to having on Saturday assaulted Annie Williamson or Jardine, his wife, in her house in St Michael's Buildings, by striking her a blow on the mouth with his fist and cutting it to the effusion of blood. The Fiscal stated that on Saturday night the accused's wife had gone to look for him as she had no money. She found him in a public house and brought him home. He laid down half a sovereign (about 521/2 pence), and on his wife asking him if that was all she had to get he struck her on the mouth. These cases must be dealt with so as to stop them. The Baillie said "This kind of thing is getting far too common in Dumfries. You must pay a fine of 20 shillings, or go to prison for a month."

In January 1906 Alexander Thomson aged 24 from Aberdeen was appointed; he was dismissed in November 1906 for drunkenness. John McClune aged 22 from Mount Pleasant was appointed in December 1906. In 1913 he resigned upon transfer to Winnipeg Police.

On 28th March 1906 the 'Standard' reported:

AN OUTRAGEOUS PRISONER

*At Dumfries Burgh Court on Monday – before Baillie Lennox – John
Burns and Edward Campbell, labourers, were charged with having
stolen ten pairs of spectacles from the person of Wm. Stewart, pedlar,
in Macdonald's lodging house in Munches Street on Saturday. Burns
pleaded guilty, but Campbell denied the charge, and was dismissed.
The Fiscal (Mr. P. McGowan) stated that only one pair of the spectacles
had been recovered. The Baillie said he would hear the next charge
against him before passing sentence. Accused was further charged with
having committed a breach of the peace and made a great disturbance
in the cells on Saturday. He pleaded not guilty to this charge. The
evidence showed that he was put into the cell opposite the door which
leads from the police office to the Town Hall, in which voting for the
School Board was proceeding; and accused began to kick the cell door
and make a great noise. He was asked by the police to take his boots off
but he refused, and they had to take them off by force. They had also to
handcuff him, but he hit the door with these, and the second time they
had to handcuff his hands behind his back. Accused said the police ill
treated him. They bled his ear and five of them smashed him with their
firsts. The handcuffs were not taken off till Sunday morning. Mr. Lipp,
chief constable, said they were taken off about 5 o'clock on Saturday
afternoon. Accused was sent to prison for sixty days for the first offence
and thirty days for the other.*

Daniel Glover aged 19 from Buittle, Dalbeattie was appointed in November
1907. He resigned upon transfer to the Glasgow City Police in December
1910, while Thomas Caven aged 22 from Corsock joined in April 1908 only
to resign in February 1909.

The Dumfries and Galloway Standard dated 13th January 1909 reported the
death of Chief Constable Lipp as follows:

"DEATH OF THE CHIEF CONSTABLE OF THE BURGH

*Dumfries is mourning the death of Mr. George Stephen Lipp, chief
constable of the burgh, which took place at his residence, Ardgowan,
Lockerbie Road in the early hours of Thursday morning, after a long
and painful illness. In the early part of August Mr. Lipp was feeling
run down, and he decided to go to his native Banff-shire for change
and rest. While there he had the misfortune to slightly injure his back,
and he returned to Dumfries about the end of August in even a worse
condition than when he left. He was only able to attend to business for
a few hours each fore-noon. Then an attack of pleurisy developed. He
was laid aside for a considerable time, but gradually improved until he
was able to take a walk round the garden. He never regained his former
strength however, and about a fortnight ago his illness took a somewhat*

*more serious turn and it was apparent the end could not be very far off.
He was able to leave his bed for a very short time on Christmas day,
and on two subsequent occasions, but at the end of the year he suffered
a severe relapse, and about three o'clock on Thursday morning there was
a decided change for the worse. He was seized with violent pain and
after much suffering he lapsed into unconsciousness. Dr Hunter was
sent for, but before his arrival Mr. Lipp had passed away.*

*Mr. Lipp, who was only in his thirty ninth year was a native of Fordyce,
Banffshire, being the youngest son of Mr. Alexander Lipp late gardener
to the Duke of Richmond and Gordon at Glenfiddich, Dufftown. He
comes of a fine stock, and his parents are both hale and hearty at the
advanced age of over eighty years. At the age of nineteen, in the year
1889, Mr. Lipp joined the Linlithgowshire police, and during a term of
nine and a half years service in that district he was stationed at Bo'ness,
Uphall and Bathgate. He also had some experience in the head office of
the Midlothian Police, Edinburgh, and being a man of good education,
his promotion in the service was rapid. He was made a sergeant
comparatively early, and on the 7th January 1889- exactly ten years
before the day of his death, he was appointed inspector of the Dumfries
Burgh Police being the first to fill that office. His quiet, unassuming
manner, soon gained for him a foremost place in the hearts of all classes
of the people of Dumfries, and many a poor creature was sent on his
way rejoicing through his kindness. On the retirement of the late Mr.
Malcolm, Mr. Lipp was appointed chief constable on 5th March, 1903,
and his term of office has been marked by a conscientious discharge of
duty, and a desire and readiness to give his assistance to all who might
require it. He performed his work to the satisfaction of all, a by no
means easy task, and was a great favourite with the bugh officials. He
acted as prosecutor in the occasional absence of Mr. Thomas McGowan,
and in that capacity also he gave the utmost satisfaction. He was of a
retiring disposition and preferred the privacy and comfort of his home
to the attractions of social functions. When his strength permitted, he
took great pleasure in working in the garden, and latterly he used to
while away the sometimes long hours by playing the violin, in which
he was somewhat proficient. He found congenial society and pleasant
recreation on the bowling green, where his presence will be greatly
missed. He was a member of St Michael's Church and there, the few
who knew him intimately were proud to call him a friend. He had
held for a number of years a position on the directorate of Moorhead's
Hospital, in which he took kindly interest. He is survived by his father
and mother, three brothers and a sister, who are all married. One of his
brothers is a grocer in Elgin, another a gardener in the neighbourhood of
Keith and the other a traveller, residing in Edinburgh.*

MAGISTERAIL REFERENCE

Before commencing the ordinary business in Dumfries police court on
Thursday morning, Baillie Macauley said he was exceedingly sorry
to hear that their chief constable, Mr. Lipp, had gone from them. He
understood it was ten years that day since he came to Dumfries. He
was a very gentlemanly man; everybody liked him; and he thought it
was their duty to express their deepest sympathy with his mother and
the rest of the family. He hoped Mr. McGowan would send a letter to
that effect, that they sympathized very much with her in the loss of her
dear son, and hoped that the Heavenly Father would strengthen her in
her severe trial.

Mr. T McGowan prosecutor, associated himself with the remarks Baillie
Macauley had made. During the time he had been Fiscal his duties
had caused him to have numerous communications with Mr. Lipp, and
he could only say that as an official he was one of the finest men he
had ever met, and as a friend he was particularly desirable. They all
mourned his loss very greatly.

Ensign Evans, of the Salvation Army, said that on behalf of the
Dumfries Company he had to say that they would greatly miss the
Chief Constable.

Mr. S Brown depute town clerk, said that he heartily concurred in the
words that had been spoken of Mr. Lipp.

THE TOWN COUNCIL TRIBUTE

Before beginning the usual business at the monthly meeting of the
Town Council on Thursday, Provost Lennox made sympathetic reference
to the death of Mr. Lipp, and moved the following resolution: "That
this council resolve to express their deep sense of loss in the death
of Chief Constable Lipp, which occurred this morning. Mr. Lipp's
faithful, honourable, and independent discharge of his duties were a
great support to those responsible for the government of the town, and
his courtesy towards everyone, even the poor and unfortunate who
necessarily came within the sphere of his duties render his loss one
which will be felt throughout the whole community. The council further
resolve that this minute be engrossed in the minute books and an excerpt
thereof sent to Mr. Lipp's relatives". He said that as chief magistrate
of the town he had great pleasure in working along with Mr. Lipp. He
considered him to be one of nature's gentlemen, and he acted in a way
which they seldom saw in anyone placed in Mr. Lipp's position.

Baillie Hastie, in seconding, endorsed what the Provost has said. There
was nothing but universal lamentation throughout the town that day,

at the death of the chief constable. Mr. R A Grierson, town clerk, said he desired on behalf of the other officials and himself to associate themselves with this resolution. There was necessarily very close intercourse from day to day between the various officials, and when that intercourse was of a pleasant character at it was in the case of Mr. Lipp it made all the difference in their daily life, and also perhaps had more influence in securing the efficiency of the system which they administered than they might think. No one who had served the town of Dumfries had desired more earnestly to live at peace with all his brother officials and to act loyally and considerately towards them than Chief Constable Lipp. Notwithstanding that, he was always actuated with the absolute independence and with a determinations to carry out his duty, and he conceived it to be, without fear or favour, and moreover he did so always with a modestly and a self effacement which, he thought, was an example to them all. It was just ten years that day since Mr. Lipp entered upon his duties at Dumfries. His stay had been all too short, but they would long remember the pleasant friendship they had with him, and the good example of an honourable life which he had left behind. (Applause). The resolution was unanimously agreed.

THE FUNERAL

The remains of the late Mr. Lipp were conveyed from his residence in Lockerbie Road yesterday afternoon to the passenger station and thence by rail to Dufftown, Banffshire, where they are to be interred today. The midsteeple bells were tolled and along the route of the processions the blinds of the houses were drawn. An escort of twelve policemen under Pipe Major Ancell, the drill instructor, preceded the hearse, and immediately behind it came the Town Council and burgh officials headed by the officers with halberds draped and reversed. (A list of all who attended the procession then follows and includes Mr. Gordon, Chief Constable of Dumfries County Constabulary and Mr. Donald, Chief Constable of the Stewartry)

A short service was conducted at the house by the Rev. J Montgomery Campbell of St Michael's Church. The coffin was of polished oak with brass mountings and on the brass plate was inscribed: "George Stephen Lipp, died 7th January 1909, aged thirty-eight years". On it rested the cap which formed part of Mr. Lipp's uniform. There were also some beautiful wreaths, one being form the burgh police and another from John C Lipp Edinburgh brother of the deceased. On arrival at the station the coffin was carried from the hearse to the funeral car by several constables who have seen the longest service including Inspector Campbell and Sergeant Kerr. The funeral party departed for the north by the Caledonian train which left Dumfries at 6:57."

There was great debate over who should replace Mr. Lipp, with a faction of the council wanting a local man, Inspector Campbell and another faction wanting to advertise for an outsider. The whole issue turned into a political 'hot potato' and the council were in turmoil over the decision.

On 13th January 1909 the Dumfries and Galloway Standard reported on the council meeting to elect the new chief constable:

"DUMFRIES CHIEF CONSTABLESHIP

The special meeting of the town council held yesterday after receiving notification of a handsome gift for repair of the Midsteeple, proceeded to consider the vacancy in the office of chief constable.
Provost Lennox said he thought they ought to remit to the Watching Committee to draw up the conditions of appointment a suggest a salary, so that it could be reported to the special meeting to be held next week to consider the Town Hall Question. He moved accordingly, and Baillie Hastie seconded.
Mr. Obrien moved, as an amendment, that the Council remit to the Watching Committee to have the position advertised, to arrange as to the salary, and bring up a report.
Mr. Connolly said there had been great crying out in this council about letting contracts to support local industries and local enterprise. Now his view of the matter was that they should not advertise at all, but ought to give promotion to our local men, men who had been in the service of the police force in this town, he understood, for eighteen years. If they appointed one of them to the chief constableship it would also mean promotion for two others.
The Provost: If you are going to discuss the general question we should go into committee.
Mr. Hiddleston seconded Mr. O'Brien's amendment and said he thought they ought to advertise the position. If they did that they did not debar the local men from applying.
Mr. Connolly moved as a second amendment that they do not advertise, and that the appointment should be from their own local force.
Mr. Dykes seconded
The Provost then withdrew his motion in favour of Mr. O'Brien's amendment.
Dean McKerrow: It Mr. Connolly's motion is carried, does it confine us to our own local force?
Baillie Macauley: Oh yes. You should make the appointment today.
A vote was taken in the form. "Advertise or not to advertise," and resulted as follows:
To Advertise – Provost Lennox, Baillie Macauley, Dean McKerrow, Mr. Dakers, Mr. Hiddleston, Mr. Irving, Mr. Kissock, Mr. O'Brien, Mr. Sinclair and Mr. Smart – 10. Not to advertise – Baillie Hstie, Treasurer Wyper, Mr. Copland, Mr. Connolly, Mr. Cowan, Mr. Dykes, Mr. Glencross, Mr. R.C. Kelly, Mr. Mogerley, Mr. Robinson and Mr. Ritchie 11.

Mr. Irving (o Mr. Connolly): Move your motion, and show your hand.
Mr. Connolly: I move that Inspector Campbell be appointed to the position.
The Provost: You cannot do that without notice. If you make the appointment today I must say things that I would rather not say.
Mr. Hiddleston: Do you think it is worth while appointing a chief constable (Laughter)
Mr. Irving: I would like to ask Mr. Connolly if he thinks Inspector Campbell is fit to take the position of chief constable? (Cries of "Oh.")
Mr. Connolly: I would like to ask Mr. Irving if he takes me to be a fool, (Laughter) I think the fact that Inspector Campbell has been in the service of the burgh for eighteen years, with never once a complaint against him, is sufficient testimony that he will be able to fulfill his duty in the future as he has done in the past.
Mr. Dakers moved that it be remitted to the Watching Committee to bring up a report as to the arrangements for the appointment and the salary before they made any appointment.
Mr. O'Brien: And fix an age limit.
Mr. Brown: That is fixed by law.
Mr. Robinson said he had his opinion on the matter, but he thought Mr. Connolly's motion simply referred to no advertising. That was his impression.
Mr. Kissock seconded Mr Dakers's motion.
Mr. Connolly asked the Town Clerk if that motion was in order after the decision come to.
Baillie Macauley said that as a member of the Watching Committee he wanted nothing to do with it now. Let the Council fix the salary then at once, and finish it when they had gone so far.
Mr. R.C. Kelly supported Baillie Macauley. From what he had heard there was a majority of the Council in favour of Inspector Campbell.
Mr. Hiddleston: Where did you get your information?
Mr. Kelly: I heard it today.
Mr. Hiddleston: Is that another English Street story?
Baillie Macauley: A Vennel story. (Laughter)
Treasurer Wyper: It is not the Vennel we are in just now. (Laughter) There seems to be two members who have voted under some erroneous impression, and I think the vote should be taken properly.
Mr. Connolly: You cannot go back on the vote. I don't care what is said about the Vennel at all; I will stick to my motion.
Mr. Robinson said that no one knew what way he was going to vote. He though it was very unfair to say anything about a majority. The inspector for a few years back had been getting £5 a year for inspecting the lighting. He thought that was one matter – there might be many others – that ought to be taken into consideration.
Mr. Irving: It seems to me that Mr. Robinson has promised to give his support to Mr. Campbell, and he regrets it now.
Mr. Robinson: I claim the protection of the chair; and I say to Mr. Irving

that is a manifest untruth.
Mr. Irving: I can hear from what you said today.
Mr. Robinson: I tell you it is an untruth, and you must withdraw it.
Mr. Irving: I will not withdraw it. It seemed from your statement today that you are supporting Mr. Campbell.
Mr. Robinson: It is untrue, and I ask you to withdraw.
Mr. Irving: I will withdraw no statement I have made today. I will leave the meeting first. I hate that hedging.
The Provost: You must withdraw a statement that you cannot prove.
Mr. Irving: I say it is clear to me. I don't say it is true.
Provost: Then you must withdraw it.
Mr. Irving: If you ask me to withdraw, I will do so from the meeting, but not from my statement
Mr. Robinson: I refer you to Mr. Campbell himself then.
Mr. Connolly: Call in the sergeant at arm. (Laughter)
Mr. Hiddleston: Go on with the business.
Mr. Irving: What I have said is clear to me that he has promised to support Mr. Campbell, and now that the Inspector has a majority he is vexed for it.
Mr. Cowan: That is making things worse.
Baillie Macauley: What way did Mr. Robinson vote?
Mr. Robinson: I voted for 'not advertise'.
Baillie Macauley: What did Mr. Connolly say? "Appoint from our own force." You voted for that.
Mr. Robinson: That does not confirm Mr. Irving's statement.
Baillie Macauley: It confirms it so far.
Mr. Kissock said it seemed that their members had voted for the wrong motion, and there must be some way of putting the thing right. The vote should be taken over again.
Mr. Connolly said this Council is not so stupid as not to understand what he meant.
The Provost said that when the motion was given by the clerk it was "advertise or not advertise."
Mr. Grierson said that Mr. Connolly's had confined them to make the selection from their own force: but if there was going to be a misunderstanding he thought the vote should be a distinct and understood expression of the Council.
Mr. Connolly said he would stick to his guns. He wanted a fair thing and he would have it. To say thay did not understand was absurd. As Baillie Macauley said, they might as well make the appointment that day because they could not advertise it.
Treasurer Wyper: Or leave it to the Vennel to make the appointment. (Laughter)
Mr. Connolly: Well, I have no objections (More laughter)
Mr. Kissock suggested that the Council should disregard this motion and remit the whole question to the Watching Committee to report, and they could then decide whether to advertise or not.

Dean McKerrow: That was the original motion.
Mr. Connolly: I maintain that you cannot do that. You are breaking the rules of all societies if you do it.
Mr. Dakers: There is no reason why you should not go on with the motion before the meeting. I am quitre clear on what Mr. Connolly said.
Mr. Kissock: But there are other members who are not.
Mr. Dakers: Well let them speak for themselves.
Mr. Connolly: Any of us who are liable to be defeated; and let those who have been disappointed take it like gentlemen.
Mr. O'Brien moved that the Council now adjourn. This was a very important matter they were considering. They were about to fill up a very important position; and he was afraid they were stultifying themselves in the eyes of the candidates for the position. He thought the Council should adjourn till that day week because he was inclined to think from the information they had before them that day that they would be better of the legal advice of the Town Clerks.
Mr. Connolly: Your motion is absolutely out of order Mr. O'Brien. You are trying to override my motion. Mr. O'Brien you are not chairman.
Dean McKerrow seconded Mr. O'Brien. A vote was then taken and the motion by Mr. Dakers to remit to the Watching Committee was carried by eleven votes to nine.

On 13th January 1909 the 'Standard' reported as follows:

"The Town Council yesterday were within an ace of appointing a successor to the late Mr. Lipp, Chief Constable, without further delay. A motion not to advertise the post, but to make the selection from officers presently serving in the force, was carried by one vote. The difficulties were raised and the suggestion was made that some members had been ready to give a merely complimentary vote for a friend but were nonplussed when they found it was likely to be an effective one. A policy of deliberation was finally resolved on and a report on the conditions of appointment is to be called for from the Watching Committee before the final step is taken."

On 16th January the 'Standard' again reported:

"Quite apart from any question as to who is to fill the position rendered vacant by the lamented death of Mr. Lipp, it would be unfortunate that the Town Council of Dumfries should feel itself fettered by what must be termed the casual vote of Tuesday. The terms in which the motions were put to the meeting were certainly not free from ambiguity, and left room for the misunderstanding which was afterwards alleged; and the supporters of any candidate would be doing him a disservice by seeking to snatch, in a preliminary round, what might appear a temporary advantage at the risk of alienating possible sympathizers.

*Besides, the motion was carried was far from explicit. The reference
to 'the local force' is a vague phrase, certainly applicable to that of
the county of Dumfries, which has its headquarters in the town, and
to that of the Stewartry, as well as the burgh constabulary. But apart
from all technical niceties, the broad principle to be acted upon is that
the council should have the opportunity of expressing a deliberate
and matured judgment on a question which will go far to determine,
probably for many years to come, the efficiency or inefficiency of one of
the most important braches of the public service; and no candidate with
good claims to the position can suffer from the fullest consideration."*

During this time for 'mature' consideration the Watching Committee received
a letter from HM Inspector of Constabularies, Major Ferguson, condemning
any consideration of Inspector Campbell as a candidate. The Watching
Committee then obviously recommended to the body of the council that the
post should be advertised and a wider pool of candidates should be sought.

On 6th March 1809 the council again met to decide on the new chief constable
and the 'Standard' reported:

"THE CHIEF CONSTABLESHIP

*It had formerly been agreed that the chief constable should receive a
salary of £200, with an increase of £5 at the end of each five years
of service. The Watching Committee submitted the following leet of
applicants for the appointment:*

*1) William Black, Assistant Superintendent Criminal Investigation and
   Deputy Chief Constable of Glasgow,*
*2) Donald Cameron, Superintendent and Deputy Chief Constable of
   Elginshire,*
*3) Alexander Duncan, Detective Sergeant Criminal Investigation at
   Govan,*
4) Alexander Christie, Superintendent, Paisley and
5) George Nicol, Detective Inspector of Edinburgh.

*Baillie Hastie moved that the Council now proceed to appoint a Chief
Constable from the leet, and Mr. Daker seconded. Mr. Connolly said
he had been very much surprised to see that they had not the courtesy
to put their own inspector on the short leet. He thought that was really
very unfair. At the first meeting they had in connection with this matter
he had made a motion to the effect that the appointment be made from
their own local force, and that motion was carried by one of a majority.
At last meeting they rescinded that resolution, also by one of a majority.
He was not going to say anything about the procedure of that meeting.
He thought it was altogether unfair. But he thought the least the
committee might have done – not only out of courtesy to the inspector,*

but also out of courtesy to one half of the Council who voted for him – that his name should have been placed on the leet, and that he should have been given a fair trial along with the other gentlemen they had thought proper to put on the leet. He knew for a fact that the inspector had the sympathy of practically the majority of the Council; while if they went outside the Council altogether and took the townspeople into consideration – and he thought in a matter of this kind they should consider the ratepayers – he did not think he would be exaggerating when he said that there would be twenty to one in favour of their own inspector. (Cries of "No, no") He considered the inspector to have been very badly treated. No doubt the letter received from Major Ferguson was very damaging, but he was very glad to say that even many member of the Council who would not have voted for the inspector did not approve of the action of Major Ferguson, and it had been universally condemned both inside and outside the town. Although the inspector's name was not on the leet the sympathy of the Council and also that of the townspeople would go out to him for the very cruel and unfair and unjust treatment that had been meted out to him.

Mr. Robinson (addressing the Provost) said he would like to know if he as Provost had received a testimonial from HM Inspector in favour of any of those on the leet or of any other candidate.

The Provost: I did not ask, sir; I have not had any correspondence with the Inspector. I have not even answered the letter that was received. I would not have it said that I was interfering in any way.

Mr. Robinson said that his question did not suggest that: It might have come as a thunderbolt. But it did seem strange to him that a man who was obviously so deeply concerned about the appointment should send a letter with such damaging effect as that regarding Inspector Campbell. It was strange that a gentleman holding such a high position should have gone out of his way to write such a letter, whether solicited or otherwise. There were two ways to look at it.

Mr. Irving (Interrupting) said this was extremely out of order.

The Provost: Let us hear what he is going to say, He is perhaps going to move an amendment.

Mr. Robinson said he did think Major Ferguson's action was universally condemned. He had gone out of his way in writing such a letter. If he had been solicited to do so he would probably have written it as a private letter; if he had not been solicited, it was going very far out of his way to write it.

Mr. Connoly: I think it is well that the Council and the public should know that it is my intention to have a question raised in the House of Commons in regard to that letter. (Applause from the body of the hall)

The Provost said if there was no amendment they would now vote on the five names submitted. Each member should name the candidate he favoured, and they would drop the one with the lowest number of votes *in turn. When the successful candidate had been decided in this way it would be moved from the chair that he be elected. This method would leave a good deal of discussion.*

Mr. O'Brien moved that they proceed by nomination in the ordinary way; and Mr. Smart seconded.
The Provost: It is a matter for the Council to decide if you prefer it that way.
Baillie Thomson seconded the Provost.

On a vote being taken, Provost Lennox's motion was carried by 18 votes to 7....
On the first vote taken, eleven votes were given to Assistant-Superintendent Black, Glasgow; nine for Superintendent Christie, Paisley; and five for Detective-Inspector Nicol, Edinburgh......
A second vote was taken between the two gentlemen highest on the leet, and it resulted, for Mr. Black 13; for Mr. Christie 12.....

Provost Lennox then moved that Mr. William Black be appointed chief constable of the burgh. He would with pleasure have moved the appointment of any one of the three gentlemen who had been voted upon. He had great difficulty in coming to a decision which of the three he would vote for as they were all equally good men. They could only appoint one, unfortunately, and he had pleasure in moving that Mr. Black be appointed.

Baillie Thomson said he had very much pleasure indeed in seconding the motion. He could have wished that the gentlemen he supported had received the majority of votes; but he cordially accepted the decision of the Council. He was sure Mr. Black would prove a worthy, painstaking, hard working chief constable, and he looked forward to his appointment as likely to be productive of very much good to the community. (Cheers.) The motion was unanimously adopted.

Chapter Ten
CHIEF CONSTABLE WILLIAM BLACK

William Black was born on 10th July 1881 at Anstruther, Fife. His father, William Black, was a constable with Fife Constabulary and his mother, Margaret Fraser or Black had married his father in 1877. William (junior) joined the Clackmannan Constabulary in 1900 and in 1902 transferred to the Glasgow City Police where he quickly rose to Detective Lieutenant (Assistant Superintendent).

Chief Constable William Black O.B.E.

He was appointed the Chief Constable of Dumfries Burgh Constabulary in 1909, aged twenty-eight years and commenced duty on a wage of £200 per annum. He was to serve as Chief Constable of Dumfries Burgh Police for twenty years and later the chief constable of the newly created Dumfrieshire Constabulary. In later life he admitted that he had applied for a number of posts away from Dumfries but had not been successful and remained in Dumfries for the rest of his working life.

Dumfries Burgh Police 1909

Rear L to R: Dan Glover, Thomas Campbell, George Carson, William Airdrie and John McClune
Centre L to R: James Thomson, Robert Broadfoot, Robert Beattie, John Killop and David Hastings
Front L to R: James Murray, Inspector John Campbell, CC William Black, Sgt John Kerr and John Dickson

The 1911 census shows that William Black, aged 31 years, lived with his wife Catherine Couston or Nivison or Black, aged 33 years, and his two step-children, Robert aged 10 years and Violet, aged 8 years, at Rockleyvale, Lockerbie Road, Dumfries. They were married at Edinburgh on 16th June 1910. William Black was awarded the M.B.E. in the King's Honours list in 1935 and the O.B.E. in the King's Honours list in 1946.

Also appointed in 1909 was George Sim Carson aged 22 from Holywood. He resigned in 1912 upon transfer to the Dumfriesshire County Constabulary.

1909 also saw William Airdrie appointed. Airdrie a 21 year old from Old Luce resigned upon appointment to the London Metropolitan Police in 1910.

In January 1910 James Service aged 19 from Auchleach, Clachanmore, Wigtownshire, was appointed. Constable Service retired in 1947 as an inspector with 37 years service. Later that year William Robinson Wilkie aged 23 from Edinburgh was appointed. He later resigned upon appointment as sergeant in Macclesfield. In December that year James Stoddart aged 22 from Lanark joined the force. He resigned in November 1915.

September 7th 1910 saw the following in the press:

"SERIOUS WIFE ASSAULT

In Dumfries Police Court on Monday – before Baillie Hastie – John Beck, ironmonger, was charged with having on Saturday, 27th August, assaulted Ann Maxwell or Beck, his wife, by striking her on the face with his fist and butting her on the face and body, with his head in his house at 27 English Street. He pleaded guilty. Mr James Kissock, procurator fiscal, stated that accused had apparently been drinking and about 10 o'clock on the night in question he went into his house, locked the door, and put the key in his pocket. After his wife had put the children to bed, he began to curse and swear, and accused her of being with another man in an ice cream shop. He struck her on the face. She ran to the door, but could not get out and she got through a window on to the roof, and dropped into the close. When she got to the close mouth there was a young woman standing, and while she was telling her story accused came down the close, seized her by the throat, knocked her up against the wall, struck her and butted her on the face and body, and knocked her down. Accused was previously convicted of wife assault on 17th February, 1909. Baillie Hastie imposed a fine of 20 shillings, with the option of ten days imprisonment."

Alexander Gibson aged 23 from Wigtown was appointed in January 1911. He was dismissed in May 1912 for drunkenness. The same year Robert Chisholm aged 20 from Kirkmichael was appointed. He resigned in August 1913 upon being offered a post with the Glasgow South West Railway.

In August1912 George Robertson Money joined the force. Money, 23, a native of Terregles, resigned in 1915.

During the evening of Saturday 9th July 1911 there was a major disturbance in the town centre of Dumfries. David Wilson, a 'Special Reservist' of the 3rd KOSB based at Hannahfield, Dumfries was found in a drunken state in High Street. Two non commissioned officers of the KOSB attempted to get him back to barracks and were conveying him along the Plainstains when he began to struggle and squirm lying down on the pavement. The trio had made their way along High Street and a large crowd had gathered observing their progress and in doing so blocked the roadway.

Constables James Thomson and James Service of the Dumfries Burgh Police being attracted by the crowd pushed their way through and went forward to help the struggling man and send him and his escort off to camp. Some members of the crown presumably thinking that the young soldier was being arrested by the police rushed the police officers and the scene quickly developed into a general melee. The two KOSB men aiding the drunk disappeared into the crowd leaving the two police officers with the drunken soldier.

Constable James Thomson

Constable James Service

The man kicked and struggled and the constables thought that it would be necessary to convey him to the police station at the town hall in Buccleuch Street. Unfortunately the crowd had grown further and they were hemmed in. The two officers struggled and managed to get the man through the crowd and into the narrow passage on the west side of the Midsteeple. Unfortunately the crowd had multiplied and was now estimated to be a thousand strong and completely blocked in the two officers and their custody.

The police officers were jostled and kicked and the surge of the crowd carried them across the roadway and into the doorway Hepworth's Clothiers at the corner of Queensberry Square. (Present day Starbucks café).

The police and their custody managed further along the High Street heading towards Burns Statue when the situation deteriorate and they became the subject of attack by sticks, stones and bottles. During this period Constable Service was struck on the neck and face.

Some of the crowd attempted to aid the police officers, but a rowdy and hooligan element attempted to again rush the police officers at Young's Corner (The junction of High Street and Friars Vennel).

Fortunately Sergeant Killop and Constable Stoddart came upon the scene and burst through the crowd to assist their colleagues. All four officers were required to use their batons during the fracas.

Sergeant Killop

Constable Stoddart

The four officers managed to get the prisoner to the station house in Buccleuch Street next to the Municipal Chambers (the then Town Hall) where the crown laid siege to the building for a short time with some threatening to set fire to the building. Chief Constable Black who had came to the entrance of the station and was met with a wave of missiles.

Dumfries Burgh Police June 1911
Rear L to R: Constables A Gibson, J Service, W Wilkie, J Stoddart
Centre L to R: Constables D Hastings, R Beattie, R Broadfoot, J Thomson, J McClune, G Carson
Front L to R: Sgt J Killop, Insp. J Campbell, CC William Black, Sgt J Kerr, Constable J Dickson

Several arrests were made by the police and the situation was eventually calmed.

David Wilson, the catalyst for this event appeared at court the following Monday and was fined.

On 19th August 1911 James Grindall a labourer 16 Queensberry Street Dumfries appeared before the Police Judge and was charged that:

"1. On August 16th in the shop at 90n High Street occupied by Adolph Young Jeweller he did assault Adolph Young by aiming a violent blow at his head with a piece of lead attached to a cord and

2. he did maliciously break and destroy two panes of glass in a show case and a pane of a plate glass in a window show case.

The accused pleaded guilty with provocation. The Procurator Fiscal, James Kissock stated that about 3:30 pm on Wednesday the accused went into the assaulted man's shop and handed him a watch which the accused said he wanted repaired. While Mr. Young was examining the watch the accused swung the piece of lead alluded to, weighing about a pound, at Mr. Young.

The lead missed the mark, however and broke a pane of glass in the counter show case. Mr. Young made to get round the counter, but before he could do so the accused smashed the other pane of glass in the show case. Mr. Young tried to push the accused out of the shop and in the struggle the accused pushed his foot through a window show case. The accused was badly cut on the right arm and had to get three stitches put in. The accused really believed that he had some grievance against Mr. Young and whether there was any real foundation for that belief was being made the subject of enquiry. Mr. Young was not hurt. Police Judge Macauley placed Grindall on probation for a month."

On 31st December 1911 Chief Constable Black's Annual Reports show the force strength as:

One Chief Constable,
One Inspector,
Two Sergeants and
Eleven constables.

The average age was 34 years, the average height 5 feet eleven inches and the average service eleven years.

*John Graham, spirit merchant, Coach and Horses Inn was in Dumfries
Burgh Police Court on Monday before Baillie O'Brien charged with*

*1. Being the holder of a certificate granted under authority of the
Licensing (Scotland) Act 1903, top keep a public house for the sale of
excisable liquor, having been found in a state of intoxication, in said
premises.*
*2. Having knowingly permitted drunkenness by allowing Adam
Dobson, foreman wool sorter, Woodside Cottage, Troqueer who was
then in a state of intoxication to remain within his premises, to which
he was liable to certain penalties and, in addition, his certificate may be
declared void and null and*
*3. On the Whitesands near the Coach and Horses Inn, assaulted
Constable George Carson by seizing him by the throat, compressing his
throat, throwing him on the ground and attempting to kick him.*

*The accused pleaded not guilty and was defended by John M Haining,
Solicitor.*

*Constable Carson said he remembered Sunday morning March 10th.
He was in Friars Vennel between 12 and one am, when Constable
Stoddart told him that there was a disturbance at Graham's house. The
witness went down to the Coach and Horses and found Mrs. Graham
outside the door, kicking it with her heel. She was crying. She was not
sober. She gave the witness certain information, and he knocked at
the door and Graham came to the door without opening it, and asked
who was there. Witness said that it was the police, and the accused
asked what he wanted. Witness asked him to open the door and allow
his wife to get in, and he said the wife was not going to get in there
that night. The accused then went upstairs and he opened one of the
windows and looked out of the window next to bank Street. He asked
the witness what he wanted and the witness asked him to come down
and open the door and allow his wife to get in. He ultimately agreed
and came down and opened the door.*

*The witness asked what was the cause of the disturbance, and the
accused said it was the wife. Witness told him he was the worse of
drink and the accused denied it. Witness said he was and the accused
called him a F****** liar. The accused and his wife then commenced
arguing and the wife went inside and brought out a fender which she
said he had broken. Witness started to walk along the Whitesands and
the accused called him back.*

*Witness went as far Mr. Wylie's door and waited until the accused came
up. He asked the witness not to report him, but the witness said he was*

going to report him. He tried to persuade the witness not to report him and then seized the witness by the throat. A struggle took place and both fell to the ground and when they were down the accused tried to kick him. Witness got on top, held him down and sounded his whistle. He asked the witness several times to let him up and the witness did so on condition that he would behave himself. Witness followed him into the house when the accused began bathing his fingers, one of which was cut. It got cut on the numerals of the witness's night coat.

Shortly after that some of the other members of the night force came up. Constable Stoddart first then Sergeant Kerr and Inspector Campbell. Witness explained what was wrong to Sergeant Kerr and the latter asked Graham what he had to say for himself. He answered that he had lost him temper. Witness went upstairs and the stairs were strewn with broken glass. A coal scuttle was laying half way up the stairs and there were coals on the stairs as well as glass. The glass panels on two room doors on each side of the stair head were broken and the woodwork of one of the panels smashed. Witness went into one of the rooms and there he found Adam Dobson, Woodside Cottage, Maxwelltown who was almost helplessly drunk.

After hearing the agents, the Baillie found the three charges proven and imposed a fine of three guineas, with expenses, or twenty or days in the jail."

| Constable Carson | Inspector Campbell | Sergeant Kerr |

During June 1913 the bi-annual census of vagrants was taken on a Sunday by Dumfries Burgh Police and it was found that there were a total of ninety vagrants in Dumfries. They consisted of:

"Three males and one female in the police cells,
Four males and two females in the infirmary and poorhouse,
Sixty-two males and ten females in common lodging houses and Three
adult males, three adult females and two female children found in the
parks.
Thirty nine males, fifteen females and two female children were
Scottish, twelve males and one female were Irish and twenty one males
were English. There were twenty three vagrants, fifty six tramps seeking
work and eleven pedlars acting as vagrants."

On 21st May 1913 Edward Ferguson, a 19 year old from Dumfries joined the force. He didn't last long as he resigned on 8th November that year. Shortly after, in September that year James Coates aged 21 from Dalbeattie joined. He had served in the City of Glasgow police from 17th December 1912 until 31st August 1913 before transferring to the Dumfries Burgh Police. In September 1914 he resigned upon joining the Scots Guards and served throughout the First World War. Upon the cessation of hostilities he rejoined the burgh force and resigned in December 1919.

On 27th September 1913 the Dumfries and Galloway Standard reported as follows:

"SON ASSAULTS MOTHER

In Dumfries Police Court on Thursday - before Provost Macaulay –
George Henderson, baker, Milton Place, St. Michael Street, pleaded guilty
to a charge of having, on Wednesday, assaulted his mother in her house
at Milton Place by striking her on the head with his fist. The Fiscal,
Mr. J Kissock, said that the accused had been drinking for some time.
Between 9 and 10 o'clock in the morning the accused's mother missed
some money from a box. She asked the accused if he knew anything
about it, and he , resenting this, became very outrageous and struck
his mother a blow on the left side of the face. He was going to strike
her again but a neighbour interfered and prevented him. Accused's
face was badly bruised, and in reply to the Provost he stated that the
bruises were caused by the police. The Fiscal: We will hear how that
came about later. He was assaulting the police when they apprehended
him. The Provost said it was disgraceful for the accused to carry on
with his mother the way he had been doing. The accused admitted
two previous convictions and with an admonition to stop drinking the
Provost imposed a fine of 10 shillings with the alternative of seven
days in prison. The accused was further charged with having assaulted
Constables Service and Clark by kicking them on the legs, butting them

with his head, and attempting to bite them while they were engaged taking him to the police office. He pleaded not guilty, and the case was adjourned until today for proof, bail being fixed at £3."

Constable Robert Martin Broadfoot

OFFICER DIES ON DUTY

On 13th October 1913 Constable Robert Martin Broadfoot died whilst on duty. A native of Maxwelltown he joined the burgh police in 1903 and had been stationed at Noblehill since 1909. He was thirty years of age and was survived by a widow and 3 year old son who celebrated his third birthday on the day of his father's death.

Constable Broadfoot was found dead outside Dumfries railway station at 10.50 pm on the pathway leading to the Lockerbie road on the east side of the station, by George Goldie a newsagent. The police doctor, Dr Hunter attended and certified that death was due to heart failure.

At his funeral, his coffin was carried by Constables Dickson, Beattie, Thomson, Service, Monie and Coates. Sgts. Kerr and Killop and Inspector Campbell under the charge of Chief Constable Black were present along with representative of the Dumfries County police and the Stewartry Police.

On 27th November John Smith aged 24 from Kincardine was accepted and in December that year James Clark a 20 year old from Forfar joined the force. Clark resigned on 8th November 1915 upon appointment as a constable with the Dumfries County Constabulary. Similarly in January 1914 Samuel Walker aged 21 from Lanark joined the burgh force only to join the county constabulary in October 1915. In a reverse of this trend, in April 1914 Thomas Thorburn Kerr served with the county constabulary from May 1913 to April 1914 before joining the burgh police. Kerr was later fined 40 shillings (£2) in November 1920 for absenting himself from duty to accept a free supper from the licensee of the Globe Hotel.

On 29th December 1913 Constable George Robertson Money resigned from the force. Below is the testimonial provided to him by Chief Constable Black:

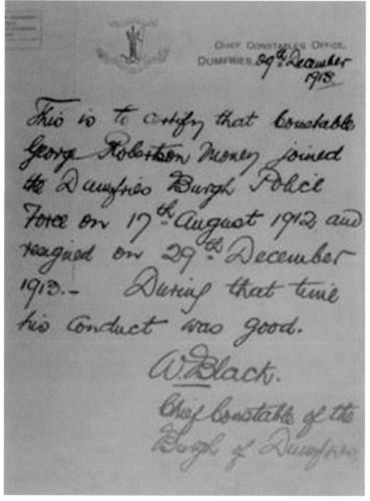

"This is to certify that Constable George Robertson Money joined the Dumfries Burgh Police force on 17th August 1912 and resigned on 29th December 1913. During that time his conduct was good."

In April 1914 Walter Scott Lochhart a 23 year old from Dumfries transferred from Ayrshire Constabulary to the burgh police and William Sharpe a 24 year old from Wanlockhead joined as a new recruit.

In October that year, George Cuthbertson a 24 year old from Kirkcudbright joined the burgh police. He had served with the Glasgow City Police between January 1913 and September 1914.

On 14th April 1915 Constable John Dickson, aged 55 years, unfortunately had to retire through failing health with 34 year's service. He was born in Tinwald in 1860 and joined Dumfries Burgh Police 1881. He served under chief constables John Malcolm, George Lipp and William Black.

Constable John Dickson

Constable Dickson was on duty in 1882 when the Earl of Rosebery unveiled Burns Statue at the junction of Castle Street and High Street and was also on duty on 20th June 1887 when the town celebrated Queen Victoria's golden jubilee.

The unveiling of Burns Statue in 1882

In February 1919 Thomas Baird aged 26 from Sanquhar joined the burgh police closely followed by Samuel Chisholm a 21 year old from Irongray. In March that year William Haining a 21 year old from Lochmaben joined up, but he didn't last long he resigned in July 1919. He was replaced by Arthur Samuel Jamieson a 29 year old from Leith Also accepted at this time was Frederick Welsh Crosbie a 24 year old from Dunscore and James Smith a 26 year old from Edzell. In August that year John McDonald a 28 year old from Erskine was accepted and a month later was joined by James Clark a 25 year old from Forfar who had previously served with the burgh police. January 1920 saw Alexander Anderson from Inveresk accepted as a constable.

June 12th 1915 saw the following occurrence:

"PRISONER'S ESCAPADE

Attempted Suicide in the Cells

Escape from Hospital

A sensational escape was made yesterday by a man named William Gemmell, who had been taken into custody on a charge of being a deserter from the Scots Fusiliers. The man's arrest was effected by Constables Beattie and Service about 7 o'clock on Thursday evening, and he was lodged in one of the cells at the police office to be detained overnight awaiting appearance before the magistrate yesterday morning. A few minutes after the man had been placed in the cell one of the constables looking through the small opening in the door discovered the prisoner lying on the floor of the cell, with his tongue protruding from his mouth. He was found to be in an unconscious condition, and while Dr. Hunter, the police surgeon was being summoned, Sergeant Killop tried to bring the man back to consciousness by means of artificial respiration. On Dr. Hunter's arrival this treatment was continued for some time, and at length the man showed signs of regaining consciousness. Gemmell had apparently attempted to strangle himself by means of his muffler, which he had twisted round the gas bracket placed outside the cell. He was removed to Dumfries Infirmary and kept there overnight, under the supervision of one of the police. On being admitted to the infirmary, the man's clothes were taken from him and placed in the lavatory. On going to the lavatory after getting up yesterday morning he apparently discovered that his clothes were being kept there, but he made no attempt to escape then. About 8 o'clock he again went to the lavatory. The policeman on duty, not suspecting the man's intentions, did not follow him. He was absent from the ward for some time, and on investigations being made it was found that Gemmell had dressed himself in his clothes while in the lavatory and made his escape by one of the windows. Search was made by the police in the vicinity of the town, but so far the man has not been arrested. The gown with which he was supplied on being admitted to the infirmary was found near to the town."

In April 1920 the following was reported in the press:

"CHARGE OF ATTEMPTED MURDER

DUMFRIES EX-SOLDIER ARRESTED

A sensational occurrence is said to have taken place in a house in Queensberry Street, Dumfries, on Saturday night, when it is alleged that a young man named Charles Johnston attempted to murder his wife by stabbing her with a dagger. The man served with the 1/5th Kings Own Scottish Borderers during the war and was married while on service with the 'Colours'. Some time ago he conducted a fried fish and potato shop in Friars Vennel, but recently had been employed as a coach trimmer at the Arrol Johnston Motor Works at Heathhall. He lived with his wife at 18 Chapel Street, but it is said that owing to some disagreements his wife left him, and had been staying with her parents, Mr. and Mrs. Mitchie, at their house at 85 Queensberry Street. It is here that the attempt on her life by her husband is alleged to have been made. According to reports Johnston visited the house late on Saturday night and tried to get his wife to come outside of the house to speak to him. She had some talk with her husband, but refused to leave her parent's house. He then went away and it is presumed visited his own house in Chapel Street. Shortly after he again returned to his father in law's house and it is alleged that he stabbed his wife with a dagger through the left upper arm, the dagger going through the fleshy part of the arm, and also piercing the breast. It is said that the man was prevented from doing further injury to his wife through the interference of her father and other members of the family, and it is also alleged that in the scuffle the man was found to be in possession of a razor. The woman's wound was dressed by Dr. Speed, assistant to Dr. Kerr, and several stitches had to be inserted in it. Johnston was arrested by the police in the house. The dagger, with which it is alleged he made the attempt on his wife's life is one with a long blade, such as carried by German Officers, and had been brought home from the war as a souvenir. Johnston is a well known junior footballer of the town."

"AT THE POLICE COURT

At the Dumfries Police Court on Monday – before Judge Hastie – Johnston was charged with the crime of attempted murder, and on the motion of the Fiscal, Mr. J. M. Haining, he was remitted to the Sheriff.

Yesterday Johnston appeared for judicial examination before Sheriff Campion on a similar charge."

In November 1923 Andrew Burns a 24 year old from Berwick was accepted while in June 1924 William John Macher, 23 years, from Forfar was accepted. In November 1925 John Nelson Wilson a 22 year old from Carluke joined the force and In February Robert Dickson Johnston aged 23 from Kelso was accepted.

1919 also saw the formation of Queen of the South Football Club. 'The Queens' were formed after a public meeting arranged to create a new football team for the town. Several names were considered including Nithvale, Southern Wanderers and Dumfries and Maxwelltown United, but the name, Queen of the South that originated in a poem by David Dunbar was chosen.

Chief Constable Black and the Dumfries Burgh Police in the early 1920's

"1926 The Coffee Close Murder

The Coffee Close ran between what is now High Street and Queensberry Street. Numerous lodgings were accessed via these types of closes and living was very cramped. In an upper flat of the Coffee Close lived a woman called Annie Mather. Annie lived there with her two children.

Annie sometimes co-habited with an English traveling showman called Arthur Pepper and it was said that he was the father of her children. Annie lived in abject poverty and in 1926, to make ends meet, she took in a male lodger to augment her income. Arthur Pepper was jealous of the lodger whose presence caused a great deal of animosity between Arthur and Annie.

On the morning of 8th February, 1926, neighbours heard screams from Annies's house and when one of them entered she saw Annie lying on the kitchen floor, bleeding profusely. Arthur Pepper was the only other person in the house at the time and, fearing that she might meet a similar fate to that of Annie, the neighbour, withdrew and informed a passing police constable of what she had seen.

The constable entered the house and found Arthur Pepper still present, near to the body of the lifeless Annie. He arrested Pepper and a search of the house later revealed a cut throat razor which appeared to have been the murder weapon. A post mortem examination confirmed that Annie's throat had been cut with an instrument similar to the razor.

At his trial for murder before the High Court at Dumfries, Pepper's defence team lodged a special defence of insanity at the time of the crime and tried to persuade the court that Pepper was not answerable for his actions as he was insane at the time he cut Annie's throat. The jury rejected this defence but, believing Pepper had acted out of jealousy and had been of diminished responsibility at the time of the crime, they found him guilty of the lesser crime of culpable homicide and he was sentenced to 7 years imprisonment. Arthur Pepper served his sentence and returned to Dumfries where he lived until his death in 1954."

Constable Walter Lockhart was second on the scene moments after Constable Kerr. Constable Lockhart noted the following in his notebook:

"Murder in Coffee Close

About 9.45 am on Monday 8th February 1926 I was in Castle Street when Edward Grant, coalman, 58 English Street, came to me and said he thought there was a murder in the Coffee Close. I went there and going up the stairs to the house occupied by Agnes Mather I met Constable Kerr at the door of Mather's house along with Pepper, I went into the house and found the woman Mather lying on the floor of the room on her back with her throat cut and a large pool of blood on the floor. The wall on the right hand side of the door was also splattered with blood and a white slip was covering the woman's body up to her neck. I could see the cut in her neck and I lifted up the slip a little to make sure whether she was quite dead or not. I saw at once that life was extinct. Constable Kerr took Pepper away to the police office and I remained in the house with the body until the arrival of Inspector Kerr and Dr. Gordon Hunter who looked at the body. They went away and I stayed in the house until I was relieved by Constable Shanks at 11.10 am."

On 18th November 1927 The Dumfries Burgh Police Force was inspected by Major W. D. Allan O.B.E., Her Majesty's Inspector of Constabulary within

Murder in Coffee Close.

About 9.45 am on Monday 8th February 1926 I was in Castle St. when Edward Grant Coulman 58 English St. came to me and said he thought there was murder in the Coffee Close. I went there and going up the stair to the house occupied by Annie Mutton I met Geo Kerr along with Peppers. I went into the house and found the woman Mutton lying on the floor of the room on her back with her throat cut and a large pool of blood on the floor. The walls on the right hand side of the door was also spattered with blood and a white cloth was covering the woman's body up to her neck. I could see the cut in her neck and I lifted up the cloth a little to make sure whether she was quick dead or not but I saw at once that life was extinct. Constable Kerr took Peppers away to the Police Office and I remained in the house with the body until the arrival of Inspr. Kerr and Dr. Gordon Struthers who looked at the body. They went away and I stayed in the house until I was relieved by Constable Sharpe at 11.10 am.

Dmr.

St. George's Hall, George Street, Dumfries. The parade comprised of Chief Constable William Black, Inspector Kerr, two Sergeants, two Acting Sergeants and ten constables. Inspector Kerr put the officers through a number of parade and traffic movements and Major Allan expressed his utmost satisfaction at the conclusion of the drill. Major Allan also scrutinised the station books and records and completed the visit stating that he was well satisfied with what he had seen.

On January 1928 Chief Constable Black issued the following instruction to his officers in the 'Order Book:'

ORDER

In consequence of the removal of a large portion of the population from the centre of the burgh to the Cresswell and Balmoral Park areas a re-arrangement of beats and a re-distribution of the force have become necessary.

The following are the new boundaries of the various beats, viz:-

No.1. or High Street Beat
Commences at No. 3 High Street (Appleton's shop), High Street west side to top of Bank Street, both sides from No. 108 (Farmers Meat Co. shop) to Queensberry Square, Queensberry Square both sides, North Queensberry Street both sides from foot of Kings Street to Academy Street east side of Church Crescent to top of Friars Vennel and all streets, closes and courts within that area

No.2. or English Street Beat.
Commences at No.1 High Street (Copland's shop), High Street east side and South Queensberry Street both sides to foot of King Street, King Street both sides to Loreburn Street, Loreburn Street both sides from top of Newall Terrace to English Street, English Street both sides to St. Mary's Church, Hoods Loaning both sides to Leafield Road, Shakespeare Street, Brooks Street, McLellan Street, Queens Street both sides to Brooms Road, Shakespeare Street to No.6 High Street and all closes, courts etc. within that area.

No.3. or Friars Vennel Beat.
Commences at a point oin the River Nith opposite Nith Street, Nith Street north side to Irish Street, Irish Street, Assembly Street to High Street, Bank Street to High Street and half way through all through going closes to High Street, Friars Vennel to High Street, Church Crescent west side to Irving Street, Irving Street both sides and in a straight line between the Moat Brae Nursing Home, George Street (which is included in this beat) to the River Nith, thence by the Rover to commencing point and all streets, closes and courts within that area.

No.4. or St. Michael's Beat.
Commences at the River Nith opposite Nith Street, Nith Street south side
to Nith Place, Nith Place both sides to Burns Street, St. Michae's Street
to Brooms Road, Brooms Road both sides to Leafield Road, Murray Place
both sides to Glebe Street, Craigs Road to Burgh Boundary to Bankend
Road, Glencaple Road, Kingholm Road to the river and by the river to
commencing point, including Dock Park and all street closes and courts
within that area.

No.5. or Milehouse Beat
Commences at Academy Gate opposite north end of Queensberry Street
thence by a straight line to River Nith at the boundary of No. 3 or Friars
Vennel Beat behind Moat Brae Nursing Home, by the river to boundary
at the Burgh boundary, following the burgh boundary to Milehouse
thence to a point near Marchmount Bowling Green, Moffat Road to
Victoria Terrace, St. Mary's Street both sides to St. Mary's Church thence
ina straight line to Newall terrace, Newall terrace to Loreburn Street,
Loreburns Street both sides to Academy Street and thence to a point of
commencing at Academy Gate, including Railway Passenger Station and
all street, closes and courts within that area.

No. 6. or Noblehill Beat.
Commences at Victoria Terrace, thence by Lockerbie Road to a point on
the Burgh Boundary of junction with No.5. or Milehouse Beat behind
Marchmount Bowling Green, thence by the Burgh Boundary to Stoop,
following the Burgh Boundary to Gateside of French, thence to the
Boundary stone at Westfield, thence in a straight line to Rosevale Street,
Aldermanhill Road to Glebe Street, thence along the eastern boundary
of No.4. or St. Michael's Beat from Glebe Street to the foot of Leafield
Road, Leafield Road both sides to St. Mary's Church and all streets etc.
within that area except that part of St. Mary's Street from St. Mary's
Church to Victoria Terrace and from Glebe Street to Leafield Road in
No. 4 or St. Michael's Street Beat.

Constables are responsible for the proper watching of all property
on their beats. Where through going closes extend from one beat to
another, each constable will patrol half of the close from his beat and
Sergeants will see that there are no misunderstandings as to which beat
constable is responsible for any particular property.

On and after 18th. January 1928, two constables will have charge of
the Noblehill district maintaining a day and night patrol alternately.

The day constable will take duty at 1 pm; and, with an interval from
5 to 7 pm for refreshment, he will go off duty at 11 pm. From 9 to 11
pm, except on the night when the night constable is off duty he will
patrol Lockerbie Road and half way down each street between Lockerbie

Road and Annan Road, St. Mary's Street, Passenger Station, Lovers Walk, Edinburgh Road and Moffat Road.

The night constable will take duty at 9pm and with an interval from 1 to 2 am for refreshment, will go off duty at 6 am. Between 9 and 11 pm except on the nights when the day constable is off duty he will patrol the remainder of the district not then patrolled by the day constable. At 11pm he will take over the whole beat as above described. Both constables will report at the police office when they go on and off duty.

Night constables who take up duty at 6 and 7 pm will not report at the police office at 8pm as formerly and will remain on their beats.

While the night sergeant ands acting sergeant are taking refreshment in the police office the night office constable will take street duty except at times when the exigencies of office duty prevent his doing so

W, Black
Chief Constable

June 1928 saw the acceptance of William Gibson a 21 year old from Ancrum.

The Police Parade and Review Magazine 12th April 1929 reported:

"Mr. William Wilkie on 1st April was appointed as Chief Constable of South Shields Police. Mr. Wilkie, a native of Edinburgh, had joined the Dumfries Burgh Police as a constable in 1910 and was the clerk in the Chief Constables office. He left the Dumfries force and was appointed Sergeant and Chief Clerk at Macclesfield Borough Police in 1918. He was later promoted to inspector and ultimately senior inspector. In 1922 he was appointed as Chief Constable of Glossop."

Constable William Wilkie:
In 1911

William Wilkie Chief Constable
in 1929

On Boxing Day 1928 Dumfries Town Hall in Buccleuch Street was razed to the ground by fire. The police office, as part of the building was also destroyed in the blaze. There is a school of thought that the officers themselves were responsible for the fire as the premises are reputed to have been virtually uninhabitable. Fortunately Chief Constable Black's office was in the Sheriff Court across the road.

It is unknown exactly how the officers managed at that time, although it has been suggested that they decanted to the cells under the sheriff court.

The Dumfries and Galloway Standard reported on the fire:

"DISASTEROUS FIRE

Dumfries Town Hall Destroyed

Valuable Pictures Saved

The Dumfries Town Hall in Buccleuch Street was wrecked by fire which broke out this morning shortly after seven o'clock. The fire must have had a good hold of the building before the discovery was made, because when the first helpers arrived flames were already issuing from the roof of the building at the side near the town clerk's offices, which adjoin the hall. The first persons on the scene were police sergeant Service, who was on duty in the police office, and Mr. T Kerr, the janitor at the Sheriff Courthouse buildings. On seeing the extent of the fire they gave the alarm, and immediately rushed up to the Town Council Chamber, where there were a number of valuable paintings on the walls, and their efforts were directed towards the salvage of those pictures, which include examples of the art of Landseer and Raeburn, valued at about £12,000, and also to the famous 'Siller Gun' presented by James V1 of Scotland to the Corporated Trades. The Town Hall was itself still in darkness and Sergeant Service and Mr. Kerr had to work by the aid of an electric police lamp. The recovery of the smaller pictures did not present much difficulty, and they were soon taken from the walls, but the large Landseer, which depicts a scene in the veldt, and the Raeburn portraits of a gentleman standing at the head of a horse, were of such size that there salvage could only be undertaken with considerable labour. The portraits of former provosts and documents were taken from the Provosts room, but the Landseer and Raeburn pictures could not be removed from the building and were placed in a corner of the Town Hall which was likely to be untouched by the flames. It was not long before the Fire Brigade was on the scene under Firemaster Thomson and four lengths of hose were connected up. As showing the extent of the fire the fire brigade were engaged for almost three hours in the work of subduing the flames.

The damage was confined to the roof of the building and a view obtained from a neighbouring building showed that the whole roof has been destroyed and only the blackened rafters remain. From the Town Council chamber there were several large gaps to be seen in the roof, and the water from the hoses had poured down into the main building, and there was a danger that many of the ceilings would collapse. The Town Council chamber has been seriously damaged by the fire and the ceiling is completely destroyed. The Provost's room is intact except for some damage to the ceiling. The water flowed to the lower part of the building and there was a great state of disorder in the police office, where documents had to be hurriedly collected and stored for safety, and the office also had to be used as a temporary store for articles taken from the other officers adjoining the Town Hall.

Much favourable comment was heard with regard to the promptness and energy with which Sergeant Service and Mr. Kerr dealt with the situation at the outset and but for their immediate exertions the damage might have been much more serious. Whether a new Town Hall will be built or not is problematical, but to restore the present building will certainly require the expenditure of a very large sum of money.

Their work was attended with a certain amount of dangers. At one period a part of the ceiling fell on the head of Sergeant Service, and but for the prompt attention of Mr. T Kerr, he might have received considerable injury.

This is the second fire which has occurred at the Dumfries Town Hall, and on the occasion of the last outbreak, twenty years ago, which was not so serious as the present one, the expenditure on the work of renovation amounted to £2200."

On the 10th May 1929 the Duke of Buccleuch officially opened the newly constructed St Michael's Bridge connecting Broom's Road, Dumfries to Pleasance Avenue, Maxwelltown.

On Thursday 3rd October the same year Maxwelltown left the Stewartry of Kirkcudbright and was subsumed by Dumfries when the burghs of Dumfries and Maxwelltown merged into one Royal Burgh consolidating the local government and community facilities. However another year was to pass until on 15th May 1930, the chief constable of Kirkcudbrightshire handed over responsibility for policing Maxwelltown to Chief Constable William Black of the Dumfries Burgh Police and Mr. Black became the Chief Constable of the Dumfries and Maxwelltown Burgh Police, or as it was known at the time, 'Greater Dumfries.'

On 5th October 1929 the 'Standard' reported on the amalgamation of the two burghs:

GREATER DUMFRIES
CELEBRATION OF UNION OF BURGHS
CEREMONY AT ST MICHAEL'S BRIDGE
DUKE OF BUCCLEUCH OPENS GATEWAY

*"The amalgamation of Dumfries and Maxwelltown was celebrated
with appropriate ceremonial on Thursday, when a number of interesting
public functions were held in honour of the important event in the
history of the two towns. Thursday afternoon was general holiday, and
both towns were 'en fete,' all the public buildings and business premises
being decorated with flags and bunting, and in the evening illuminated
with the very effective colour schemes. Delightful weather favoured the
outdoor ceremonies, and the bright sunshine added to the general gaiety
of the occasion.
St. Michael's Bridge was the scene of the principal ceremony of the day,
and there before a crown of some ten thousand townspeople the Duke of
Buccleuch, Lord Lieutenant of Dumfriesshire, opened a gateway which
had been erected between the two burghs, symbolical of removing all
barriers to union. Through the opened gateway the town councilors of
Maxwelltown marched, entering into the larger burgh in which their
town in now incorporated. At this ceremony, very appropriately, and
important part was given to the children, who are the future citizens of
Greater Dumfries.*

*In the evening the Freedom of the United burghs was conferred on the
Duke of Buccleuch; the Rt. Hon. William Adamson, Secretary of State
for Scotland; and the Rt. Hon. Sir John Gilmour, former Secretary of
State for Scotland, at a great meeting in the Drill Hall, which was
attended by an audience numbering close on four thousand.*

*A dinner was given in the Assembly Rooms at the conclusion of the
Freedom ceremony, at which three hundred guests were present. Sir
James Crichton-Browne, the oldest Freeman of Dumfries, proposed the
toast of, 'The United Burghs,' in an entertaining speech, 'embroidered
with fantasies,' giving an account of a meeting on the Old Bridge of the
Lady Devorgilla and Sir James M. Barrie.*

*As a spirited and enlivening conclusion to a great day in local annals,
there wqs a remarkably fine display of fireworks on the Millgreen."*

The real catalyst for the change was not a change in heart by the burgesses
of Maxwelltown, who had always dismissed amalgamation in favour of an
independent burgh, but a change in law whereby burghs with a population
under 20,000 were to be disadvantaged by the removal of some of the powers
of the councilors and magistrates. So by popular acclaim both burghs voted
for amalgamation and the joint burgh, having a population in excess of
20,000, was safe from further penalty.

Maxwelltown had been under the jurisdiction of the chief constable of the Stewartry since 1890 and had no independent police force. When Chief Constable William Black took over responsibility for the policing of Maxwelltown a number of police officers were transferred to the burgh force from the Stewartry.

In May 1930 William Mowbray Boyd a 21 year old from Troqueer transferred to the burgh police from the Stewartry force. He had served with the Stewartry from 16th December 1921 until 16th May 1930 and when Dumfries and Maxwelltown amalgamated he transferred forces. Similarly William Broadfoot Gilbert a 24 year old from Croyden, Surrey, transferred from the Stewartry to the amalgamated Dumfries and Maxwelltown force. Halbert Jamieson aged 24 from Borgue and Alexander Gillespie Wright aged 20 from Troqueer also transferred from the Stewartry to the new Dumfries and Maxwelltown police force.

The amalgamation helped the Dumfries burgh police as well. They had no station house as the old one at the town hall had not been replaced, so Chief Constable Black transferred the burgh police to the Maxwelltown Police Station and Courthouse in Terregles Street, where they remained until the new Dumfriesshire Police Headquarters at Loreburn Street was completed in 1942. The Maxwelltown Police Station and Courthouse had been built by the Stewartry Police in 1893.

In 1930 John Thomson Sandiland a 21 year old from Abernethy was accepted, as was John Anderson Sturrock, a 21 year old from Leith. Later that year John Scott aged 23, from Edinburgh joined and in 1931 James Patrick Fallon a 23 year old from Edinburgh was also accepted.

On 17th April 1932 the 'Standard' reports on a meeting of the Dumfries Town Council:

> *"DUMFRIES TOWN COUNCIL*
>
> *Amalgamation of Services with County*
> *Police force to be consolidated.....*
>
> *Dumfries Town Council decided at a special meeting yesterday to combine with Dumfriesshire County Council in the carrying out of various public services. The chief services affected by the agreement to amalgamate are the Police Forces, Library and Medical Officer's Department.....*
>
> *The amalgamations come into operation on May 15th.....*
>
> *Police Amalgamation*

Maxwelltown Police Station and Courthouse

The Provost, dealing with the draft agreement for the consolidation of two police services of the burgh and the county, made a long explanation, in which he endeavoured to show the economies which would accrue and the efficiency to be gained by unified control. The proposal before them, he said, briefly was that the two police forces be consolidated under the 1857 Police (Scotland) Act, and that in future the police administration should be carried out by a committee of the County Council, on which for that purpose to Town Council would be represented. There would be ten members of the County Council and five members of the Town Council on that committee. The basis of expenditure would be that after all annual expenditure had been ascertained and full credit given for all income, the balance would be got by two thirds from the County and one third from the Burgh. With regard to the terms of the agreement, there was a question of the value of the police stations, houses and lock ups throughout the county. The value that had been agreed on was at the sum of £20,000. From that £20,000 would be deducted a sum of £8,000 still remaining unpaid. Leaving a sum of £12,000 of which the Town Council would come under obligation to pay the County Council one third or a sum of £4.000. With regard to a headquarters police station, which would be within the burgh of Dumfries, provision was made for the cost of that station being met on the same proportions as the other costs, namely, two thirds to be paid by the County Council and one third by the Town Council. Provision was already made for all the procedure regarding the selection of the site. He would point out that under the terms with regard to the police stations and houses the arrangement would be that the Burgh would pay to the County £4,000 and the County would apply that sum towards the cost of the new headquarters.

Those headquarters had been fairly modestly estimated to cost about £12,000, so that by the burgh paying one-third of that, their proportion would be £4,000 and the County's proportion £8,000. That meant that when the Burgh paid £4,000 as their share of the police stations and houses and £4,000 as their share of the headquarters the burgh's total payment under these two heads would be £8,000. Proceeding, the Provost stated how the financial arrangements would be reversed in the case of a dissolution of the two forces taking place at any future date. Dealing with economies the Provost said that under the heading Chief Constable it was calculated that the saving as between the two Chief Constables, one for the burgh and one for the county, would be £811 per annum, and it was also stated that this combination would result in the necessity of one inspector fewer and two constable fewer, which represented a saving of £941. There was one item not estimated at all, and that was pension liability for these three men. That was stated to amount to several hundreds of pounds, so that the total estimated saving, without taking into consideration the pension liability amounted to £1600. Taking that several hundred pounds, it was estimated that *it would come pretty well up to £2,000, of which the burgh would save one-third. Further, in regard to the burgh officials who would have their work undoubtedly lessened, but whose salaries they could not very well reduce, the county would become liable to the burgh for a requisite proportion of these salaries, and on a twelve and a half years basis it would come to a sum of £1475.*

It would, in his opinion, add very considerably to the efficiency of the force, and it would not take anything away from the powers of the magistrates. They would still have the same power over the police as they had at present. He was altogether satisfied that this was a consummation which would be in the clear interest of both the burgh and the county, and would make for definite saving. The alternative would undoubtedly be, if they continued with their own police force, that they would be forced in the immediate future to erect a new headquarters for the police, and that the cost could not be much less than the sum he had already stated, £12,000. The burgh would have to bear the entire cost of that, and on the whole he put it to them that that was an agreement, which they would both do well to enter into in the interest of both the burgh and the county ratepayers, and he therefore proposed that the agreement be ratified, and that power be granted to sign it.

Treasurer, Dinwiddie in seconding, said he considered the views of the Town Council had been very carefully considered and carefully guarded and every provision made. With regard to the site for the new police headquarters if they did not approve then they had an opportunity a selecting a site of their own, and if they did not approve of the accommodation the matter could be placed before the Secretary for Scotland whose decision would be final. The economy to be effected would be very considerable by reason of the amalgamation itself, and it should be further borne in mind that if they did not amalgamate there was a very heavy expenditure which they would require to meet in regard to the new buildings."

There was great debate over the proposed amalgamation which at one stage was called 'glaringly one sided' and slewed in favour of the county council. However, on April 27th 1932 the Dumfries Burgh Council voted 12 to 6 in favour of the amalgamation of two police forces, and the die was cast for the creation of the Dumfriesshire Constabulary.

In 1932 Chief Constable William Gordon of the Dumfries County Police retired and the new Dumfriesshire Constabulary Police Committee had to choose a new chief constable for Dumfriesshire County and all the towns, villages and burghs within Dumfriesshire, Annandale and Eskdale.

Dumfries Burgh Police Force 1932 on the date of the amalgamation with the Dumfries County Police
Rear L to R: Constables J McDonald, W Sharpe, A Wright, A Burn, J Fallon, W Boyd, J Sandilands,
F Crosbie, J Sturrock, W Machar, W Gibson, W Gilbert and H Jamieson
Centre L to R: Acting Sgt J Clark, Constables W Lockhart, J McDonald, A Jamieson, J Smith, T Kerr and Acting Sgt Chisholm
Front L to R: Sgt J Service, Insp. J Kerr, Provost Brodie, Chief Constable William Black,
Mr. R A Grierson (Town Clerk) Mr. A P Hannah, Convener of the Watching Committee, Sgt J Thomson

The 'Standard' report on 18th May 1932:

"CHIEF CONSTABLSHIP

Mr. William Black, M.B.E., Chief Constable of Dumfries, on Monday took over his new duties as Chief Constable of the consolidated police forces of the County of Dumfries and the Burgh of Dumfries, his appointment having been unanimously agreed at a meeting of the Joint Police Committee at the County Buildings on Saturday.

Mr. Black has discharged his duties in the burgh with much satisfaction since coming to succeed the late Mr. Lipp as head of the police force, and his promotion to take charge of the larger force throughout the whole county is well deserved. Mr. Black was honoured three years ago when his name appeared in the King's birthday Honours list as a Member of the British Empire.

A native of Anstruther, Fifeshire, Mr. Black had a legal training on the staff of the Town Clerk of Dunfermline, which proved very valuable to him in later years. He served for a period in the Clackmannanshire police force at Alloa, and was then transferred to the Glasgow force. There he spent a few months in the Chief Constable's office and was then chosen for duty in the detective department. Promotion came rapidly, and he became Detective Inspector, a rank which is now designated as Detective Lieutenant. |When he received his appointment to take charge of the Dumfries force, Mr. Black was chief indoor officer in the Criminal Investigation Department at Glasgow.

Mr. Black has always striven to keep down crime and offences by preventative methods, and in particular to keep children away from moral contamination. In the late Provost McGeorge's time he began the practice of bringing youthful offenders up before the chief magistrate in a private room, where they were cautioned and sent home. Mr. Black has from the first taken a deep interest in the play centres movement in Dumfries, and has been an active assistant in organizing summer galas for school children."

Mr. Black was to serve as Chief Constable of the new Dumfriesshire force from 1932 until 1948 when the Wigtownshire, Stewartry and Dumfriesshire forces were amalgamated to form the Dumfries and Galloway Constabulary under the leadership of Chief Constable Sidney Arthur Berry.

Chief Constable William Black of the newly formed Dumfriesshire Constabulary.

After retirement William Black OBE moved to Ancrum in Roxburghshire. He died of a coronary thrombosis, aged 77 years, on June 5th1958 at his home at Ancrum. He was preceded by his wife Catherine, who died on 24th April 1952 of a cerebral thrombosis at Galashiels Hospital.

Dumfries Burgh police force ceased to be in 1932, but the following Scotsman article from 1933 is worthy of note. John Kerr served as constable, sergeant and then inspector in the burgh force for a total of 36 years before the amalgamation with the Dumfriesshire County force.

6th March 1933:

POLICE INSPECTOR RETIRES;

Inspector John Kerr, Dumfries Burgh Police

"Inspector John Kerr is to retire from the Dumfriesshire Constabulary after 37 years service at Dumfries. In consequence of his retirement, Office Sergeant Walter Hogarth, of Dumfries Headquarters, has been appointed to take charge of the Dumfries Sub-Division, including the burgh of Dumfries and the landward part of the district. Office Constable John McDonald has been promoted to be Office Sergeant, to be stationed at Dumfries Headquarters."

Acknowledgements

There are a number of people I would like to thank for their help, encouragement and support for this project:

My good friend: retired Glasgow Detective Inspector Joe Craig, Curator of the Dumfries Police Museum for his incredible knowledge of historical police information.

Retired Dumfries and Galloway Constabulary chief constables: David Strang and Patrick Shearer, together with their deputy chief constables Bob Ovens, George Graham and Mike McCormick for their support and encouragement.

Thanks are also due to Police Scotland, in particular Chief Superintendent Kate Thomson, Divisional Commander, Dumfries and Galloway Division for access to the Dumfries and Galloway Police Museum and its police records and museum artifacts.

To Alison Burgess the staff at the Ewart Library in Dumfries with particular thanks to Cathy Gibb for her help and good counsel in developing the book. Special thanks to Dumfries Library Archivist Graham Roberts, for proof reading and historical guidance.

Thanks are due to the Friends of the Archives for their unstinting work in retaining and understanding our history and supporting me in the project. Also thanks to another good friend, David Kirkwood, retired superintendent and author of the 'Wigtownshire Police,' for his encouragement.

Fiona, the saint that I married, is blessed with endless patience as over the years I seem to have spent more time reading and writing that I ever intended, but she has always been there for and with me, so she gets a very special mention.

The book is dedicated to everyone who served with the Dumfries Burgh Police. There were no women officers or staff named as there were no women in the police back then, but behind most of the men was a mother, wife, sister, daughter or partner who kept them right, so the book is dedicated to them as well.

The Author

John Maxwell is a retired police officer. He spent thirty five years with Dumfries and Galloway Constabulary as an officer and as a member of support staff. Born in Dumfries and a qualified engineer, he joined the police in 1978 and commenced his career at Castle Douglas before moving onto Dalry, Dumfries, Locharbriggs, the Lockerbie enquiry, Thornhill, the Procurator Fiscal's Office and the Force Control Room at Cornwall Mount. He served his final two years of police service as an inspector seconded to the Association of Chief Police Officers for Scotland (ACPOS) training staff in intelligence and information management.

John Is married to Fiona, they have five children and four grandchildren. He is afflicted with an unfortunate addiction to playing golf badly.

Bibliography

1) A History of Dumfries and Galloway, 2nd Edition, Sir Herbert Maxwell, 1900.Blackwood & Sons, Edinburgh,

2) The Growth of a Scottish Burgh, G.W. Shirley, Thos. 1915, Hunter, Watson & Co, Dumfries,

3) Galloway A Land Apart, Andrew McCulloch. 2000 Birlinn Ltd. Edinburgh, ISBN 1 84158 027

4) Crime & Punishment in Dumfries and Galloway 1780 - 1920, Dumfries and Galloway Library Services, Ewart Library, Dumfries

5) A History of the Scottish Borderers Militia, the Rev. Robert Weir MA 1877 The Herald Office, Dumfries

6) History of Dumfries, William McDowall, 1867, fourth revised edition with supplementary chapter by Alfred Truckell, TC Farries & Co Dumfries.

7) The 3rd Statistical Account of Scotland for the County of Dumfries, 1962, George Houston, Collins, Glasgow.

8) Dumfries Burgh and Dumfriesshire County Council Committee Minutes, Dumfries Archive Centre.

9) The Dumfries County Commissioners of Supply Minutes, Dumfries Archive Centre.

10) Chief Constables Reports 1890-1895, Ewart Library, Dumfries.

11) The History of Sanquhar, James Brown, 1891, J. Anderson, Edinburgh & Glasgow.

12) Scottish and Universal Newspapers

1721	the Dumfries Mercury
1773 - 1777	the Dumfries Weekly Magazine
1777 - 1831	the Dumfries Weekly Journal
1809 – 1884	the Dumfries and Galloway Courier
1833 - 1843	the Dumfries Times
1839 – 1884	the Dumfries and Galloway Courier and Herald
1833 – 1835	the Dumfries and Galloway Herald
1843 -	the Dumfries & Galloway Standard and Advertiser

13) Stewartry of Kirkcudbright, minutes of the Commissioners of Supply.

14) The Wigtown Free Press.

15) Dumfries and Galloway Notes and Queries, Edited by Charles Mackie, 1913, Courier and Herald Press, Dumfries.

16) The Police Scotland Museum Dumfries.

17) All Manner of People, the History of the Justices of the Peace, Johan Findlay JP, 2000, the Saltire Society. Edinburgh. ISBN 0854110763

18) The Statistical Account for Scotland, Volumes IV and V, 1791 - 1799 Edited by Sir John Sinclair, EP Publishing, 1983. ISBN0715810057 and ISBN0715810049.

19) The Encyclopedia of Scottish Executions, Alex F Young, Eric Dobbie Publishing ISBN: 1 85882 049 9

20) Dumfries and Maxwelltown Amalgamation, Historical Souvenir Illustrated Oct. 1929, Thomas Hunter & Co 1929.

21) Dumfries Story, David Lockwood, 1988, TC Farries & Co, Dumfries.

22) The Burgh Police (Scotland) Acts and other Acts of the UK Parliament.

23) Lay Justice, Bankowski, Hutton & McManus, 1987, T&T Clark, Edinburgh. ISBN 056729 139 1

24) The National Library for Scotland, Edinburgh

25) Scotland's People, National Archives of Scotland, Edinburgh

26) The Municipal Chambers, David Lockwood 2010

27) The United Burghs of Dumfries and Maxwelltown, Courier Press, High Street, Dumfries 1929

28) Tolbooths and Town-Houses, RCAHMS, Edinburgh 1996